Pedigree, Education and Deed

Saurabh Kishore Singh Sharma Sinha

Copyright © Saurabh Kishore Singh Sharma Sinha 2024
All Rights Reserved.

ISBN 979-8-89277-980-7

Pedigree

The child Saurabh Kishore Singh Sharma Sinha alias Chhotu, Great Great Great Grandson of Shri Dhanka Singh, Great Great Grandson of Shri Chhote Singh, Great Grandson of Shri Rambadan Singh, Grandson of Shri Yougal Kishore Singh (Married in Biharsharif) with Shrimati Savitri Devi, Grandson of Shri Nawal Kishore Singh, Grandson of Shri Bhim Singh, Grandson of Shri Musan Singh, Grandson of Shri Rajdev Singh (Reader at Civil Court), Grandson of Shri Bhim Singh, Grandson of Shri Balmiki Singh, Grandson of Shri Gaya Singh (Married in Sheikhpura), Grandson of Shri Vidya Sagar Singh, Grandson of Shri Ram Naresh Sharma, Grandson of Shri Rajendra Prasad Sinha, Grandson of Shri Tikkar Singh, Nephew of Shri Sachidanand Singh (Married in Amba), Son of Shri Shri Chunnu Singh alias, Shri Bibeka Nand Sinha (Married in Dharaut) with Shrimati Sunita Prasad Sinha alias Sunita Singh, Director of Bharat Institute of Engineering and Technology, Director of Bharat Pvt ITI, Director of Bharat Nursing school, Director of Bharat B.Ed college, Director of Bharat Public School, Director of Bharat Institute of Technology and Management, Director of Bharat Caring Center, Director of Bharat Builders, Nephew of Shri Murari Singh (married in Bakhtiyaarpur), Nephew of Shri Tripurari Singh (Married in Sigma), Nephew of Shri Gauri Shankar Singh (Married in More) with Shrimati Reena Singh, Nephew of Shri Bhopal Singh (Married in Pandarakh) with

Shrimati Juli Singh, Nephew of Shri Sanjay Singh, Nephew of Shri Ashok Singh [Biharsharif], Nephew of Shri Ashok Singh [Beguisrai], Nephew of Shri Kheerkhiri Singh, Nephew of Shri Shankar Singh, Nephew of Shri Rajeev Singh, Nephew of Shri Punpun Singh, Nephew of Shri Bipin Singh, Nephew of Shri Navin Singh, Nephew of Shri Dhruv Kumar Singh, Nephew of Shri Shyam Sundar Singh, Nephew of Shri Surya Narayan Singh, Nephew of Shri Pramod Singh, Nephew of Shri Chhote Singh, Niece of Shri Balram Prasad Sinha, Niece of Shri Mithilesh Prasad Sinha, Having a warts Shri Ashok Singh (Banaras), Niece of Shri Chandan Singh, Niece of Shri Sanjay Prasad Sinha, Niece of Shri Sanjeet Prasad Sinha, brother of Shri Lucky Singh married in Ramdiri, brother of Shri Alok Singh married in Maranchi, brother of Shri Azad Singh, brother of Shri Sumant Singh, brother of Shri Anant Singh, brother of Shri Guddu Prasad Sinha married in Jahanabad, brother of Shri Rajnish Prasad Sinha married in Beguisrai, brother of Shri Sonu Singh married in Banaras, brother of Shri Rohit Ranjan alias Bittu married in Biharsharif, brother of Shri Raushan Singh (Rajasthan), brother of Shri Raushan Singh (Bhopal), brother of Shri Sunny Singh, brother of Shri Summy Singh, brother of Shri Vishal Badan Singh alias Golu, brother of Shri Abhishek Singh alias Raja, brother of Shri Anand Singh, brother of Shri Chhotu Singh (Banaras), brother of Shri Chhotu Prasad Sinha, brother of Piku Singh, brother of Devi Jiya Singh, brother of Kanahaiya Singh, brother of Shri Sunny prasad Sinha, brother of Shri Shubham Sinha, having some more studying abroad, elder sister Shrimati Anjani Prasad Sinha married with Shri Venkatesh Prasad Sinha, elder sister Shrimati Rupam Singh married in Beguisrai, elder sister Shrimati Anupam Singh, married in Beguisrai, elder sister Shrimati Rakhi Singh, married in Bakhtiyarpur, having elder sister Shrimati Reshu Singh, married in Purnea, brother of Devi Shivani Singh, brother of Devi Shanu Singh, brother of Devi Deepshikha Singh, having niece Shri Chiraag Singh, and a nephew Shri Reyaansh Singh alias Suryaansh Singh, from the family of "Brahman Bharadwaj Bhumihaar, Chidaai Pariwar", having two monasteries in Banaras and a temple established in Beguisrai by guardian's, having a company named Hotcart, in which, having Apna Paints, Ferric Automobiles, Sinhaji.Com, and Apna Transport, is here to communicate with readers or followers, owners, employees, and others who could understands "English".

Education

Education means a system. A system where honesty is expected from everyone. A system that is used for making honest personalities. A system, which teaches children to opt for reading and writing for establishing communication. The first thing inside the school, any child learns, is that "Honesty is the best policy". Having any degree doesn't mean that they are an educated person. Having a degree and abusing, shouting, where it is taught, to make "Pin drop silence", then, are they any educated person? The child has a friend, has no degree, but made a drone, a flying machine, by himself. The degree is like an Empathy mapping certificate, lobbing certificate, Experience certificate, or acknowledgment certificate used for playing with the eyeballs of readers, or companies. Every day, there are new challenges, and with new challenges, new experience comes. A person who achieved a degree in graduation or a master's, but didn't apply anywhere, and lived his life on grand guardian's property, or farming or rent earning, then whether that person was educated or groomed in that field or sector? The degree means, the candidate has been groomed in that particular field or sector or had given their time in that particular field or sector, where the institution assures others. A single written complaint over any degree holder spoils their degree, experience, and other qualifications. A single written complaint over any educational center spoils its image. Earning from rent is also work, farming is also work, in that effort is given. People invest their money, and time, do labor then earn, and live politely with polite people.

The child visited Ideal Children High School, Raghunath Prasad Sharma Public School, Budhhiya Devi Public School, Patna Muslim School, Raghunath Prasad Sharma Institute of Technology, and then Fortune Institute of International Business. Among all, The child personally liked Ideal Children High School. Then liked the environment of Raghunath Prasad Sharma Institute of Technology. The child also visited IASE University, Churu, Rajasthan, then had visited Alagappa University, Karaikudi, then had visited Periyar University, Salem, had visited Vinayaka Mission University, Manonmaniam Sundaranar University, Tirunelveli, I.M.E India, Mumbai, then had visited Shobhit University too.

Whether for establishing any teaching center, or any educational center, permission or affiliation is expected? Are they both educated, who gives permission, or who expects permission? Students who learned "A, B, C, D, E, F, G, H, I, J, K, L, M, N, O, P, Q, R, S, T, U, V, W, X, Y, Z" in "Charwaaha Vidyalaya", are any fool? Respected Dr. Avul Pakir Jainulabdeen Abdul Kalam Azad, the missile man of India, studied under the street light, the street light was his table lamp. He was the person, who changed the security strength of the country. Permission or affiliation is like a trick for any bribe. No child or human can be disturbed for any bribe, or extortion, until and unless their circle, of relatives and friends feels jealous, as jealousy is a human's nature. If relatives and friends are good, then who will disturb them? If relatives and friends are bad, then, whether anyone need to disturb them?

Whether anyone needs to feed them, or whether anyone need to rob them? Where it is taught, that "India is my country, and all Indians are my brothers and sisters", there whether anyone needs to rob or to feed anyone? Police are also relatives, and thieves are also relatives. They are users of different words.

> ➤ Bribe or extortion all are forbidden earning which earns curse.

Affiliation or Permission, means, to have assurance, that, they will even care for them. Inside the system, if there is corruption, anywhere, then, there is no learning. That system is the system, which is like garbage or the worst system. For affiliation, for affiliating any institution, different agencies, expects what? For writing the letter of appreciation, expects what? If anywhere, previous year's assignments are sold, then which system were they running? What were they teaching? What students were learning, and will teach what and will serve what? Whether they learned even to write any application? Corruption endangers their own children's life and future. For instance, there was a person, from Bihar, who had rape cases, murder cases, robbery, extortion, and other charges. After every crime, he took bail using an advocate's face. He was unable to earn, using writing or reading activity. He accumulated millions of crores, and in last, his child died in a car accident. Children's marriages were not happening. That is why, it is said, that, if the child is good, then why to accumulate wealth, he will earn by himself. And if the child is bad, then why to accumulate wealth, he will spoil or will sell all one day. The child is the real property of anyone. Words are used for blessing and cursing too. Blessing has its effect, then whether cursing will have or not?

Guardians are in another cube or curdle, children are in another cube or curdle, and in that curdle, their world lies, marriage, happiness, and sorrow, happen in their curdle only. They try to addict their children to reading and writing activities, and that's why they send their children to school.

Why does, any books are praised, or worshipped? Because every book is a set of different dead pasts, which will be found to occur again in the future, because of the "Word arrow". Word arrow" keeps them alive, using the reader's mouth and their surroundings, considering them to be the variables of those books,. Wherever those variables were yesterday, we are today, and someone else will be tomorrow. Suppose, The child stopped reading newspapers, the world stopped reading newspapers for a year, or over a year, then which politician, which actor, which player, which company remained alive? Newspapers, and media, uses civilian's eyeballs, and leave them to gossip among themselves and plays with their ears, sometimes even plays with their sentiments. It is like beating "Civilians" and leaving them to shout or gossip among themselves. Because they feel that they have any power. They should understand, that they have nothing, except responsibilities. The day, when civilians will change the channel, will change the newspaper, TRP will decrease. They uses their addiction to watching television, or reading the newspaper, and show whatever, they feel necessary. Advertisements are paid, majority of news is paid. Press conferences are paid. In printing a single newspaper, there is an expense of more than rupees fifteen, which is sold in rupees five, that means, the whole expense of printing the newspaper, comes from the pocket of the advertiser, from the pocket of paid news. That means the newspaper is also like a daily magazine only.

Every day, a new customer comes, and every day new reader comes. That means, the child who took birth, in 2025, is a bigger "child", than those, who took birth in 1990. 1990's children are listening, to complaints, action, and suggestions of society over any act by different Idols of society. That means, readers are reading and their children are reacting to those stories, and are taking action over those complaints.

One very common thing, in the educational system, is that some targeted children are awarded "FAIL" on their mark sheet. What is "FAIL"? "First attempt in Learning". But, it is a trick to provoke them to suicide or to use their weapon, to earn, for answering in their own words, to show their talent. Children are taught that "Bhagat Singh" died around the age of 25. Not even seen the face of "Sataisa". If anywhere, anyone dies, then because of fraud, or cheating, from the girl. The boy trusted the girl, and the girl's mother became the answerer. The calf trusted the heifer, and the cow started answering, in such case, whether the calf would die or not? If schools are teaching, that, "Bhagat Singh" died around the age of 25, not even seeing the face of "Sataisa", then they even should teach, that Sita died around the age of 42-45-50 not even seeing the face of menopause. As a part of the Ascetic act, because, whatever happens inside the school, is also an Ascetic act, for example, Marksheet is also an Ascetic act, Shri Narendra Modi, even if were poor on his mark sheet, was called "Malechh, Lafua,

Kutta, Shuddar, Maa Ki Gaali, Mental, Fail, Rascal, Bhaduwa, Fakir", where "Sieve curses the winnowing basket which in itself has seventy-two holes", "Thief scolding the police" and Even a child was also called "Malechh, Lafua, Kutta, Shuddar, Maa ki Gaali, Mental, Fail, Rascal, Bhaduwa, Beggar" by Ascetic peoples. Lots of people did suicide, in such a behavior, inside the coeducational system. But, Whoever ate the spices, felt the spices. There was a child, studying in Banaras, Mr. Bamula, who committed suicide, after getting a "FAIL" on any piece of paper, where everyone knows, that, even after getting a degree, have to earn experience, in that field or sector. That means words hurt. Somewhere, someone intentionally tried to either kill, or provoke to suicide, or someone tried to use his nearby person for abusing and disrespecting too, that Oh, you "FAILED". Teachers are getting service charges for giving services, considering teaching to be also an act of "Service sector" their students "FAILED"!!!! In what he what he "FAILED"? Whether he "FAILED" in listening to the story, or "FAILED" in writing the story? Whether he "FAILED" in copying, or "FAILED" in "Answering in his own words"?

➤ What is "FAIL"?

The teacher raided copies of students and turned them into a raid, the moment students left them, the student opened their mouths about the behavior, of the environment inside that educational system, which turned into a raid over that educational system. When anyone gets awarded, when anyone gets first, then the whole batch sights are robbed. Inside the educational system, the height of molestation is that, girls in the old days were not allowed to read and write, later they started reading and writing, and after that, they started teaching too. Danced, abused, slapped, according to them, what is the education system?

➤ What is raid inside the education system?

The moment, any child shared his experience, that turned into the raid. The teacher raided student's copies and did "FAIL/Pass", whereas, the student raided, which turned into lockdown, somewhere.

The child mate a money lender, who collects 4% per month, which means, rupees forty thousand per month, for rupees ten lakhs only. That means, in a year, he expected four lakhs eighty thousand as interest, that means, in two years, expected rupees nine lakhs sixty thousand. That means, in around twenty-five months, collected rupees ten lakh, but still their principal amount was as it is as it was. Where banks say, that will double the amount in more than seven years, there, some expect their amount to double in twenty-five months only. Whether the government of India earns 48% on any business every year? What is the G.D.P. of the country from independence? Whether the government of India, ever had seen the face of a double-digit growth rate? The day, when these black marketing will close, that day, India will be the center of growth.

The child got a chance to visit some colleges. About one college, Management was using the same premise for running Law College, and was running CBSE school too. Was teaching Law, breaking the Law, as the same premise can't be leased for two purposes. Whether the same girl can marry two or more persons?

That will give several diseases, not only to them but even out of society. Same country, can't have two national flags. The child again visited an educational system, where management constructed the building on the land which was allotted for making the drainage system for the society. The child again visited a college, where management expected students from all over the country, but had no Hostel facilities at all. That means they were using different media, for fooling and playing with the eyeballs, and ears of children and their families, and were careless, about the weather's effects on children. How, children would be living outside the premises in winter, rain, or summer? How they would manage their early morning breakfast, to arrive at college, early morning in winter, or during the rainy season. When expecting students from other districts or states or countries, then, any college should take care of their accommodations, and meals too. The child went to a college, where, the management, intentionally "Failed" students for having more "Examination fees", and for selling assignments of previous year's students, to have some more earnings and for fooling AICTE and UGC. Teachers are also considered to be the face of god, and such things don't suit any god. But children are the face of god, anywhere. Children are the future of the country, and teachers are sculptures of that future. Teaching comes under service sector, whether for same service will anyone pay twice or thrice?

4% per month rate of interest was collected from civilians from "Fakir's" employee's doors. All's son either died, or some lost their hands, some lost their legs, some lost their others, and some became mentally retarded. Because, India pays 0.5% per annum to Japan as an Interest, and in the local market, the same money is circulated using "Fakir's employee's" face on over 48% per annum. How is it possible, that, top management is, was not knowing? For making them "debt slavery" somewhere. The child is communicating using the language "English", which means, more than 50 countries can understand, the scenario, For making them "debt slavery" somewhere and Employees were selling their time to "Fakir" and their product to "Civilians". How "Japan" would be feeling, when they come to know, that, the money they lend to any "Fakir", the same money is circulating in local market on 48% or even more, in the local market, using their employee's faces? Double business. Double cross. Ditching owner and civilian too. Fooling owners and civilians too. Civilians are the owners of their time. While pulling blood earning, sweat's earning, people earn disrespect and curse. While stealing blood or sweat, women give birth to children, as "Makardhwaj" taken birth from the sweat of "Vaayu Putra Hanuman". He is still alive, because he touched his father's feet, but "Karan" died. 4% rate of interest or even more, are expected by, them, who don't believe anything wrong in "Love" before marriage, which earns a curse in all aspects. By, employee. By, them, whomever, the government trusted. leeches of drainage, who don't know the tradition, or the marriage acts, and always interrupt with their existence. Lots of temple priests are Sc/St, maybe because of being "fed up" with Brahman's. Whether ever anyone thought, about how "Brahman" would feel, when, they read that "Ravan" died, all his sons died, every year. Ravan, great-grandson of Bramha died. Whether anyone thought, that, who are those? Ravan was also Brahman.

Wherever Ram will be, Ravan will be there by nature. If Ram is truth, then "Ravan" is also a truth. Illiterate people are expecting a 4% rate of interest. Who doesn't know that Shani Dev changes place. It is said, that "Ravan" keeps "Shani Dev" under his feet, and it is also said, that "Ravan" was very big "Pandit", he was that big "Pandit" who doesn't know that "Shani dev" changes place. Barbarik is still there. No one dies ever, wherever, "Karan" was before, there is someone else who is "Karan" today, and someone else will be "Karan" tomorrow. Wherever "Abhimanyu" was earlier, someone else is there as "Abhimanyu" and someone else will be tomorrow.

The child mates two well-known finance companies regarding vehicle finance. One is Tata Motors Finance, and the other is "Hinduja Finance". Tata Motors finance financed a commercial Tata vehicle. That means they financed to buy their product. They financed around Rupees Four lakh fifty-eight thousand only to a customer. For buying a vehicle of around Rupees six lakh sixteen thousand only. On behalf of Rupees six lakh sixteen thousand, the company collected over Rupees eight lakh ten thousand, and receipt of Rupees fifty-five thousand was in the dashboard of the vehicle. Which was paid, till before the loan completion period. That means, for buying the vehicle of Rupees six lakh sixteen thousand, the customer paid Rupees eight lakh and sixty-five thousand only. Company after collecting the amount, Auctioned the vehicle, registration number BR-01GH-3361. That means they sold the same vehicle to someone else. And collected over rupees twelve lakh over the vehicle, of rupees six lakhs and sixteen thousand only. The customer felt cheated by the company. He requested the company to either return the vehicle or return the money. Employees of the company threatened the customer, and said, that they were from any "Khaderan Singh's family". The customer went to the civil court for justice. And raised the question, that "If any company, can sell, anyone's property, or vehicle even after collecting the payment, then whether the court, whether the bank can sell their company or not, after collecting the loan amount of over thousands of crores pending over them in "Kaudi" only? As already had collected the amount. When the court said, that, no one can sell anyone's property, bought on even a "Loan", then how anyone dared to sell those property? Are they any literate people?

And then, about the "Hinduja Finance". They financed a bike, they financed the amount of around Rupees Two lakh twenty-five thousand only. The vehicle was of around Rupees three lakh thirty-six thousand only. the registration number for the bike was BR-01EF-8093. For which the customer paid around rupees two lakh ten thousand only. That means paid over fifty percent. That means paid around sixty-six percent of the payment. Till Covid-19. Now, whenever customers went, to them after Covid-19, they started saying that would have to check, whether, the vehicle was there or had been auctioned. Court ordered that, no financer can sell, anyone's vehicle or property bought on Loan. That customer was fooled to roam this office to that office. Whether that customer's money, whatever he paid, should be returned with interest or not? "Finanacer's" money has values, whether his money has values or not.

On rupees five hundred, booking happens, there even after paying more than the price, even after paying sixty-six percent of the payment, his vehicle was sold.

This is how some finance companies were fooling the customers. Which is also an offense. During COVID-19, which was an epidemic, the market was closed, and shops were closed, from where they would repay? The customer expected his money back. It is taught in Masters of Business Administration about "Moral Values" inside business. Whether morality say, to sell anyone's property? Are they literate? If customers will start buying vehicles on loan and will sell to third parties, by themselves, then will it be "Okay"? If the bank collects their money and sells their company, then will it be Okay?

The child mate a builder and his family. They constructed an apartment, on conversion, on the land of Shri Kant Singh, on trust. That, they will earn something, as laborers work on farms of some other land owners, like that, even they worked. Their children, themselves created a disturbance during construction with their presence and delayed the project. Their nature was to disturb builder, for capturing their investments, and for delaying the projects only. They already had done this with some previous builders too, with their act, which the builder's family did not know while taking on the project. And they even showed arms, for threatening the builders. Builder, anyhow constructed the apartment, having twelve flats, Six offices, twenty-two shops, and a Godown. They created a disturbance and then expected a penalty. Sometimes they abused the secretary on the site, sometimes they beat laborers, and they threatened guards. And delayed the project. Sometimes take names of some criminals, who neither can't write even an application or can read, and threaten the builders. And Shri Kant Singh became the "Dhritraashtra" of that project. All his children, disturbed, the builders. And, only created a disturbance, with their presence. Builder's children, served water on the construction, either on plasters, or on bricks construction, or ceiling construction, or any construction, but they never. Their presence meant that only disturbance would occur. The whole family of Shri Kant Singh, was only disturbing the builders. After constructing the building, they again started shouting, for disturbing them. Rather than allowing their share to be sold, they started tricking for giving money on interest. If builder would have sold their property, on time, then whether they ever would have to take any money on interest for their survival? They didn't give their right but expected to take money on interest, work on that money, and pay them, monthly. They expected someone to nurture, to train, to care for them, or to feed them. Whoever cared for them, bit them, whoever nurture them, disrespected them, whoever trained them, they robbed them only, whoever fed them, used that energy over them only. The biggest trainer of any child, the biggest carer of anyone is school, then father and mother, then those "books", including "holy books". The right to sell the property was, is, and will always be with builders and their families only. No one will buy those shares. Whether, their guardian sent their children to school, for learning the same, whatever they do? Whatever they do, their children will be found doing the same, somewhere, as the biggest nurturer, trainer, and carer, of their children are they themselves. What would be the interest for those shops?

Whoever is expecting an interest over government circulation, The child expects "Surya Dev" to do the justice. Whoever is using someone else face to run such businesses, the child expects "Surya Dev" and "Devi Bhumi, to do justice. The child from the family of Brahman Bharadwaj Bhumihaar expects from "Devi Bhumi", Please, make them "Landless, Powerless, Speechless, tongueless, handless, legless, wordless, teeth less, Navel less" considering them to be improper, for society. Prays to Vulture, Prays to Snakes, prays to scorpions, prays to leeches, prays to frogs, prays to tigers, prays to foxes, prays to deer, prays to peacock, prays to ants, prays to mice, prays to elephant, prays to dinosaur, prays to cows, prays to buffalos, prays to dogs, prays to cats, prays to lizards, prays to horses, prays to camels, prays to giraffe, prays to leopards, prays to bears, prays to kangaroos, prays to monkeys, prays to mongooses, prays to pig, prays to the eagle, prays to the falcon, prays to swan, prays to crocodile, prays to spiders, prays to the tortoise, prays to octopus, prays to bats, prays to owl, prays to snails, prays to parrots, prays to the penguin, prays to whale, prays to lion, prays to Hippopotamus, prays to all birds, prays to all fishes, Prays to all land animals, Prays to all water animals, prays to all flying animals, prays to all animals, prays to lord Pashupati Nath Paras to do the justice. After all, all humans are children of animals. Got human birth, after crossing all eighty-four lakh lives. As, they are unable to earn, from their "Laxmi", that is why, they are looking for someone who could earn from that "Laxmi" for feeding them, somewhere, for nurturing them, somewhere.

The child was running a business of wall putty, plaster of Paris, and White cement. In this regard, his truck was coming from

"Rajasthan" to "Patna". The excise department's employees expected bills from the transporter. They presented the bill to them. After that, after some discussion with the driver, they expected a penalty, because the date loading was mismatched with the date of the shipment, due to some of mechanical fault and imposed a penalty of 200% over the goods, and the importer paid. The customer paid rupees one lakh forty-three thousand extra as a penalty, even after paying all taxes. Will earn 10-15%, and pay 200% as a penalty, this is how "Fakir's" employees were running their businesses, pay 15-20 times of the total profit of that truck, because driver from Rajasthan was not comfortable in making communication with that literate excise department's worker.

Will sell what? Time are sold? Words are Sold? Employee are selling their time and services. Natural products are sold, manufactured products are sold, in whichever act "Sweat" comes that are sold. The business, that is done while threatening, that business is called robbing, and that money is called extortion money. The business, that has abusive languages, that business is not any business. Employees are better than those, who are lending their "Laxmi" on interest for their survival. At least they are selling their time. They are those, whose time has value, but, those who are using their "Laxmi" on interest, their, "Laxmi" has values only, they have no values. That means behind such business, somewhere, "Laxmi's" very big hand is there. And that is why, is expected from Lord Vishnu, to see the condition, of civilians. "Laxmi" means, brother of Lord Ganesha. That is why, it is expected from "Lord Ganesha" to see, the condition of civilians, where Bankers are corrupt. From where do they get so much money, that become "Money lenders" in society? What "Laxmi" has done? Which business is "Laxmi" running? The child expected a loan of rupees two lahks only from the Bank, where, the government of India shouts about "Mudra Yojna", but no bank gave him. His rupees Eleven thousand and forty-six from account number 30348025096 were stolen, from SBI, and no one gave any answer. Neither the manager nor customer care. Which service do they give? Why the child will ever trust any Bank? Specially government bank? Why?

Teachers are the guardians of orphan children, in the education system. They educate them, so that, they can become a nice person. They educate them, so that, they won't find to be robbing, threatening, misbehaving, or shouting with anyone.

➤ What is the result?

In the life of a hundred years, which child passed at the age of 10-12, and which child failed at the age of 10-12? Because, their students learn, that "India is my country and all or in underage or as juvenile Indians are my brothers and sisters". And, that is the place where "Shani Dev" is used for decorating results of children. Whatever happens in life, whatever any human gets, happiness or sorrow, behind that, god has their strategy, humans are fools, they don't know the future, and see the past, to understand the strategies. Whatever happens, happens for goodness, and considering that, live happiness and sorrow. God gives happiness for taking an examination of humanity and gives sorrow, for giving lessons, for giving them tuition. Never be arrogant.

While molesting "Shani Dev", Evil Ravan, earned arrogance for their family. In the fight of "Evil" and "God", only "God" will win. Inside the coeducation system, "Evil's" and "God's" children both come.

Whoever says, that they don't believe in god, that means, somewhere, they don't believe in themselves. God lies in every life. God lies in all five elements, god lies in them too, whoever says, that they don't believe in god.

Shri Narendra Damodar Das Moolchand Modi, even though he was poor on mark sheets. But, given the right to do "Mann ki Baat". While doing "Mann ki Baat" he engages all to listen to him through television, which is a talent. Every person is a talented person. The child achieved first class in Engineering, in almost boy's college, but, The child doesn't know A, B, C, or D of Urdu. The child earned third division, second division till ninth, in coeducation, but achieved first division in tenth, studying in the individual educational system. In post-graduation, The child mate a faculty, who was studying for a Ph.D. and was of age over 50. His children might have completed their Ph.D. A child scored over 90% in tenth but did not know about computers. A batchmate earned over 90% in tenth, but does not know "Sanskrit". Yes, of course, that child is good in other papers, but, the child who failed in all subjects, but was Charles Babbage of computers.

What is the degree? Just an acknowledgment certificate, lobbying certificate, experience certificate, or literacy certificate, which helps others to understand the personality, for their startups, or can be said an illusionary paper, used for playing with the eyeballs of the reader. In the nursery, some students are rejected by some schools, seeing their guardian's earnings. Whether that child failed or the guardian failed? Or, the school was running something else business, rather than educating? Or school was checking something else in that child?

Schools, colleges, universities, and institutions all are the places, that are governed for educating children. Education starts from cradle to bed to Chair and vice-versa. My grand guardian was able to read the Ramayana without spectacles only. Early morning walks and yoga were his exercise, that made them connected with their family.

There are my two uncles, Shri Ashok Singh, and Shri Kheerkhiri Singh, Son of Shri Nawal Kishore Singh, who are farmers, and milk cows on their own. Milking cows, riding horses, petting dogs, or petting animals are some exercises that make humans healthy.

People are not ruined because of their incompetence or incapability, they are ruined by seeing the progress of others. Jealousy is human nature, gossiping is human nature. Gossiping can be an act of "complaining and appreciating" too. "Complaining means discouraging, whereas, appreciating means encouraging". "Gossiping means, tricking for spying" somewhere. Gossiping or complaining or discouraging about whom? Encouraging whom? Provoking whom? In writing communication, answers should be in writing only.

Fighting is human nature, whether in speaking energy is used or not? Whether in writing energy is used or not? The whole act of

Mahabharat, or Ramayana was the act of human nature, provoked by girl, and her suggestion makers.

Some people are masters in selling their compulsions, reading and writing acts, which were designed for establishing communication with deaf and dumb children, but, they sold their compulsions. Who came first, and who did fail doesn't matter to the child, If the child is deaf and dumb, but, has a manufacturing company. But, the child is deaf and dumb. Reading and writing communication is that communication, which is for establishing the communication and keeping the silence. Who came First, who did Fail, he doesn't know. The person, who is of no use to him, will always be found to be making his "mockery" only.

A few years back, The child met his father's teacher, at a marriage party. He was the King of that Party. Motivators of that party. The child liked him at that party.

For teaching, permission is needed? For affiliation, permission is needed? Bank finances a project, sees the project and Ideas, and takes risks after understanding the project, and Ideas. Post affiliations are given, seeing the project. India got a new "Sansad Bhawan", which was working on the same premise, that Britishers made on farmer's land. That means, Post-affiliation was given to the country. Like, there is the term "Provisional Certificate".

In even Banks, there are corrupt people. People expect Banks, that they will finance their projects, that they will finance their Ideas, but, for financing any project or Idea, they expect a bribe, and that is also a reason, why, people move towards private money lenders or suicidal acts, or are doing "Debt slavery". Those, who can't help on bad days, of anyone, they even should not think of any help from anyone. Bank is for whom? They earn interest from customers. If, anyone expected a personal loan or business loan, then whether did anything wrong? Loans are for whom? The bank's business is providing loans. Not only credit cards. Credit cards have a heavy rate of interest. Suppose the child used a credit card, having a limit of Rupees fifty thousand. And repaid the amount in two years. Then, the total amount became more than around rupees one lakh. But, if the child takes a loan, personal loan, or business loan, then, the total amount to be repaid, became around rupees sixty-five thousand only in two years. Then what is a credit card? And what is business? The government expects civilians to do transactions through bank accounts only, but, they are facilitating what? As, told earlier, from his savings bank account number, 30348025096, SBI account, Rupees Eleven thousand and forty-six were stolen. Which, either was known to the customer or the Bank? Which safety are they given?

Disrespecting earns disrespect. "Sieve curses the winnowing basket, which in itself has seventy-two holes". "Thief scolding the police".

Every appreciation is not an appreciation, it is just motivation, or sometimes it can be a trick of paying down some points, encouraging someone else, or tricking for robbing someone else virtue, for being in that field or sector. Work for the same field or sector.

Interest money, over-interest money, robbed money, and extorted money, all are black money. That means, from that money, can't buy property, nor can buy any vehicle. The day, when all black money, got deposited into the government bank account, Salaries will increase, jobs will increase, and business opportunities will increase. Citizens should become honest by themselves. Government means, your child. Fooling the government means fooling your child. Child is the future of your business, in his feet, his future lies. That means, upcoming children, will have their future, their children, and their family, in their feet only. That means, the upcoming Aja, will have their "Dashratha" in their feet only, which means, the upcoming "Dashratha" will have, their Ram in their feet only.

The best example of a robber being robbed is that, whoever used water in milk to increase the quantity, became slim. Fats are barely visible. Cows even need service. The cow needs walking too, but, feeding should be in their clean utensils, made of cement, hard to move. They even need care. They have no brains. They are mammals. They have brains, have sentiments, but only for their children. They care for their children. It is said, that a cow stole the milk for her child, which is like a thief scolding the police. Humans are stealing the milk and saying, cow stolen the milk. The cow is also like a mother. For saving the calf, and heifer, they are separated after their birth.

Animals are also life, they should be respected, for their work. They understand human language, and human even understands them. Worships them. Cow is worshipped on "Govardhan Puja". Animals have saved human lives a lot of time, and will always be found saving them, by their nature. They are more sentimentally attached to their human.

Snakes are considered to be the most venomous animals, but, even they don't disturb humans, by themselves. They are those things. They are also a creature. Killing even a snake earns a curse. Snake has saved Vishnu, Snake has saved Krishna, Snake is also a creature, who had been found saving humans in the direction of Lord Shiva only. Killing even Snake earns a curse from all gods. Because they are also in their chess cube. In their own curdle. Because even snake have given their contribution in building humans.

As, many readers of any news, or any line, or any paragraph, or any page, or any book, or any article, that much people worshipped that news, that line, that paragraph, that page, that book, that article. Mimicked the same, whatever the writer wrote, and made that statement to be stronger and stronger. Like "India is Great", "*Bharat is Great*", "*Bharat Mata Ki Jai*", and "*Vande Mataram*". That means, the reader even read the same "*India is Great*", "*Bharat is Great*", "*Bharat Mata Ki Jai*", and "*Vande Mataram*".

There is an equation of "**Trigonometry**",

Sin	Cos	Tan
Perpendicular (P)	Base (B)	Perpendicular (P)
Hypotenuse (H)	Hypotenuse (H)	Base (B)

That can be easily *memorized,*

Pakistan (P)	Bhukha (B)	Pyasa (P)
Hindustan (H)	Hara (H)	Bhara (B)

Whatever the missiles, and weapons, India or Pakistan uses over each other every year, at that expense, more than a hundred colleges and universities can be established.

Now Bharat has that much power, that can pull China on their feet. China became the hub of carbon, and Bharat became the hub of farming, the hub of manufacturing, and the hub of technology. Bharat means India, which means Hindustan. In some fields, Bharat is ahead of China. The majority of Chinese don't know the easiest and preferred language, English. China is killing its citizens, by producing carbon and spreading it around.

India is surrounded by water, having long rivers and ponds, which means having great resources of fish and seafood. Fish farming of India is famous in Japan. Fish are exported all across the world.

Whether ever, anyone heard, that Bharat, India, Hindustan, captured anyone's rights or property? Whoever expected partition, whoever expected whatever, Bharat, India, and Hindustan served them. The cheapest and safest satellite launching facility is provided by India, Bharat, and Hindustan. Whether, from over thousands of years, has anyone ever heard, that, India, Bharat, or Hindustan, ever tried to capture anything or attack anyone?

➤ What is the photo?

Suppose he is a child, for him every word is a "*Photo*". The school, the question paper, where it is asked, to "answer in own words", where every word is "*Photo*", every book is a photo. Even "0" is a photo, "." is also a photo. Even silence is a reply, then answer, who passed, and who failed, where "*FAIL*" means "*FIRST ATTEMPT*

IN LEARNING". The marksheet is also a photo. Even after achieving a degree, people give services in their field or sector and then earn experience. Even after achieving the degree of P.hd, some are proven to be terrorists. The degree doesn't declare that, they are any educated, honest personalities. Letters "A, B, and C" are also a photo. Its teacher who teaches the pronunciation to children. And "*Guru Dakshina*" is their right, and respect is their earnings. Photo is also a painting, used for playing with the eyeballs, which means the mark sheet is also a painting, which means, the letter is also a painting. This book is also a photo, and the Marksheet is also a photo. Even the child has decorated some words, assembled some words, especially for the coeducational system, with a prayer, with an expectation of great success for the book. Every book, every photo, every words, are also face of "*Lizard, or Snake*", which changes colors. Read this book, five times only, first time, you will witness something else, second time, you will witness something else, third time you will witness something else, fourth time, you will witness something else, fifth time, you will witness something else. As, in manufacturing human, "*Lizard or Snake*" even had blessed.

No one ever dies, wherever we are today, someone else was ever before, and someone else will be tomorrow. India gained independence from Pakistan, and Pakistan gained independence from India. Both are still learning "*English*". Independence is like Partition. The day, the partition was held, the same day, they became independent. Both have their flag. India have their own "*Tiranga*". Both have taken Independence from each other, and Both have taken Independence from the same girl.

Employee, means, every civilian is an employee of their country. Even businessmen are paying taxes for the development of the country. Taxes are like salaries for the country, which are used for the further development of the country, either while constructing, roads, dams, hospitals, institutions, colleges, schools, universities, monuments, or power grid. Labor payment comes from the tax collected from taxpayers. Employee payment comes from the tax collected from taxpayers. Tax is the salary in the system for their services.

Never curse anyone, it earns the same. Mirror talks with mirror. Mirror said to mirror, that due to you my name defames, mirror replied, that if due to me, your name defames, then, don't look at me, look something else.

Migration affects earnings. Migration means a new startup, someone fooled someone, and compelled them to migrate. Migration means disturbance. Migration happens due to bad rulers. But, that is good, that lizards and Snake showed their face, and robbed only startup earnings, and earner migrated to seeing their nature. Migration means someone disturbed them, robbed them, that much, that, they migrated, seeing their nature. Someone robbed their "*Land, ornaments, respects, property, vehicle, health, wealth, sweat, virtue*", and then, disturbed them, so much, that, they migrated and chose the path of living alone somewhere. Given nothing, but robbed only. Whoever is found to be robbing, they are an "*Evil*" group, they are only "Gambling" in their life. Evil is also gambling using the phrase "*I love you*", the day, when, they will get slapped, the day when they will feel, the "*Gajraj's*" blessing, they will come to know, that, inside "*marriage*" groom touches the feet of his father-in-law, then his father-in-law touches his groom's feet, after having all swore. Then *"love"* can be expected. Not before that. Who came sleeping using someone else face, and used the phrase *"I love You"* over anyone?

The home, which has a grand guardian, that home remains healthier. Grand guardian, have their own experiences, and their circle.

Cheating, and copying, have no learnings and conclusions, of their own. Cheaters are always found to be cheating and copying, asking, and having no future. I need to establish communication, keeping *"pin drop silence"*, which means, through writing, then will can copy patterns from different books, but can't copy the whole conversation. Need to learn to assemble words, according to my learning. In an examination, student should hide and write, allowing someone to cheat or to copy, affects their result too. "Answer in your own words, or can be said, *"Mann Ki Baat"*.

Every countryman is an employee of the country. Till then, there is "Laxmi" and a source of regular earnings, or ideas or products that have buyers, till then, they have employees. The child only expects civilians to work hard for themselves, in whichever field or sector they are. The writer is also a laborer, working for the necessities of life. Writers are also paying taxes.

➤ Why does anyone go to school college or university?

For learning reading and writing. Reading and writing are two works for which anyone goes to school. Students go to school, for especially to learn the basics of writing, or can be said to learn assembling words. In India, Below 50% of people can read any application. Below 25% can write any application in 2025. The child is happy, that he is a writer. If he begs, then who begs? Writers are not supposed to beg. He is independent in writing. If he is independent, then readers are also independent. If he is a slave, then readers are also slaves. You are independent, that means I am independent. Mirror talks to mirror. Write and read. If anyone even has to abuse, then write on paper, read yourself, and judge, who abused whom? As the sieve curses the winnowing basket which in itself has seventy-two holes. If suppose, he begged and earned, then whether in that, anyone will expect tax or extortion? People should feel ashamed when they can't write any application. What they are, if can't write any application? Shouting puppet? If the tongue is chopped then will do what? Guardian, ever sent them to school or not? Paid fees for what? If, can't know to write to establish communication, then, whether fingers should be chopped or not? Whether those hands are given for what? Are those hands any decorative pieces? Is this whole body any decorative piece? Having "Skull" over shoulders? Why do guardians pay fees while sending them to school? Why? Whether they dried ghee in cow dung's cake?

Books of history, and Holy books, are almost the same things, having different variables, where no one dies ever. Wherever, we are today, someone else was ever before, and someone else will be tomorrow. Earlier Shri Mohandas Karamchand Gandhi did fasting, then Shri Anna Hajare did fasting. Fasting is done, for hurting "Ram" or "child" of home somewhere, for his kind sight. No work dies ever, no words die ever. Living on fast is also a weapon somewhere. It is like neither will eat nor will allow to eat. Every act or work remains alive. Every word remains alive. He can give "Dakshina" for reading his written copy, for reading his written books, not for reading other's copy.

"Sieve curses the winnowing basket, who in itself has seventy-two holes", and "Thief scolding the police".

The moon shines with the shine of the Sun and makes an eclipse on the sun. Moon means, girl. Girls from the coeducation system, are mainly shining by robbing the shine of the "Sun" or "Son", and making eclipse on "Son" only.

Always be truthful. Always be honest, always be kind, and feed hungry people, in their blessing, heaven lies. Mother and father are important things in life. Grandfather and guardian are ornaments of any family. Guardians, grand guardians, are like shields for any child.

For teaching, for accrediting, for affiliating, wherever, affiliation, or permission, is expected, that means, something is wrong. That means someone is shouting, and breaking the "Pin drop silence", That means, someone is corrupt in the system. The corrupt system always results in loss in all aspects. Honesty means free and transparent work. For, mark sheet, for affiliation, for justice, whether anyone has to bribe anyone? Wherever a bribe is expected, such a system collapses. Their children can't freely say that their guardians are this. Suppose, The child is the chief minister of Bihar or the Prime minister of the country. Who doesn't know his salary? How much he earns, who doesn't know? In a general election, more than, three thousand crores are spent, and the total salary amount for five years is around Rupees eight hundred and twenty crores only for whole 543 seats, different parties, or Private limited firms, play rummy of over rupees three thousand crores, for those rupees two lakhs fifty thousand only? In establishing, a college, school, university, or company, management takes loans, and works hard as any labor, then establishes a college, school, university, or company. If will pay bribes, then will be found to be corrupt. If anyone paid a bribe, to establish any petrol pump, then would be found robbing in the quantity of petrol. As, much honest top management will be, that much honest the system will be. Good products have lots of customers.

There is a person, who was called the "businessman of death", in Indian Politics. There is another person, who was called "AK 47" in Indian politics. There is another person, who was called "Bhishma Pitama" in Indian politics. Bhishma Pitama, the term in itself says a lot. There is an agency, who is called "Ravan" in Indian politics. There is another person, who is called "Van Diesel" in Indian Politics. There is a state, which was also called "Jungle Raaz", and there is a woman, who is also called "Surpankha" in Indian Politics. There is a person, who is also called "Pappu" in Indian politics. Words are used, or fed by their neighbors or relatives or close one's to civilians.

I don't support toxic businesses or prostitution businesses. Those businesses, can't be expressed inside school, by their children among their friends or teachers. Children should feel proud while describing their guardian's profession. Shri Narendra Damodar Das Moolchand Modi motivates civilians while describing himself as to be son of a "tea-seller", which is a good thing. Always be proud while introducing their father. His father is that teacher, who gave tuition and earned rupees three hundred per month, from two students. That means, rupees one hundred and fifty only from each. That means earned rupees five only from each student, for giving service per day, for an hour or over an hour. In that, rupees ten, daily, he fulfilled his family's needs. Always feel proud of the guardian's profession. I had seen or witnessed, that, someone, telling, that is from "Falana" family. Hided father's profession. If hided father's profession, then hided his all sacrifices. It is like any girl said, she is from "Falana Rapist family", and hided her father's profession. Like Sita's farewell held from "Ravan's door, but was of "Janak's" family. That means, Ravan was only a distraction, or was a character used for playing with others somewhere. Because girl are only a puppet, and, the girl father and groom have to touch each other's feet. Whether anywhere "Janak" touched the feet of Lord Shri Ram? Vibhishan touched. Whatever Shri Narendra Damodar Das Moolchand Modi, will be, but he can't hide, all the sacrifices of Shri Damodar Das Moolchand Modi.

Where children have their sentiments with the "Land" where they have taken birth, the land having their wardship with that child, wherever they have taken birth.

Education teaches, "Honesty is the best policy". Honesty means, being honest, with yourself.

Wherever, the phrase "I love you" gets passed easily, there, they should be asked to tell their past in present for future. 99.99% will be found to be telling their story of an adult movie. And

0.01% are those, who will be found to be using the same phrase over someone else after being rejected or even accepted, until and unless someone not asks them to write their biography or converts that phrase into marriage, where, girl father, even have to touch the feet of his groom. It is mainly that phrase, which are used by Evil's groups provoked by girls. Whether Lord Shiva did "Love marriage"? Whether Prabhu Shri Ram did "Love marriage"? Whether Lord Ganesha did? Leaves to all girl's father's to decide, that whether, they will ever touch those feet, who, are accused of making prostitutes in their past? They are those, who tries to eat someone else virtue, and themselves becomes innocent, while doing Ascetic acts. While suggesting over every act, considering girls to be cow, and everyone knows, cow have no own brains. They are like tape recorder, whatever seen in past, will implement the same, that means, will implements mistakes also. That means, if their respect was robbed, then, their daughter's respect will be robbed, if they had surgery before marriage, then their daughter will also do the same. If seen "*Jenau's*" act for their brother, then will expect "*Jenau's*" act too for their children. They are those cow. "*Jenau*" is like half murder of child, somewhere.

The phrase "I love you" is that phrase used for making Prostitute or Bhaduwa, used by Prostitute or Bhaduwa only somewhere. The moment, the writer was writing, where was "Sita/Sati"? What she was doing? Girls are considered to be face of "Saraswati". Where was those faces of "Saraswati", when the writer was writing? What is "Love"? On the one hand, they provoke the phrase "I love you" and on the other hand, expect to give in writing, as the writer wrote. Girls are only an illusion.

They have no right to face even any interview, what is coeducation? What they are reading? What are the old days? Next year, whether people will celebrate "*Ram Naumi*" or not? What is the old generation? Especially "Dancing and singing puppets", whoever will be in their whirl in the coeducational system, will become "Bhaduwa" by nature. They are those special characters. Whoever girl, has a brother in their home, stay away from there. They will be found to be selling their girl in last because they are only playing rummy, that whether "love" is "true" or "false"? This year, the Anaya baby was loved by "*Vicky*", next year with "Maninder", and after that "Ranjeet" came. They are those special characters from ancient history. And you will be found to be losing a family member from behind, and respect. They are those things. They are only entertainers. They can't be any homemaker, they will be found to be home burners only.

The child prays, that whoever finds listening to the story, to be reading the story, would be found to be living a happy, good sense and prosperous life, and blessing lies in their groom's feet only. Only the groom can give a "Long, Prosperous and happy life". Not, anyone else.

The child prays to "*Surya Dev*", the child prays to "*Shani Dev*", the child prays to "*Vishnu Dev*", the child prays to "*Lord Ganesha*", the child prays to "*Agni Dev*", the child prays to "Bramha", the child prays to "*Vaayu dev*", the child prays to all planets, the child prays to all starts, for the healthy life of Shri Bibeka Nand Sinha, Alias Chhunnu Singh, considering that clap doesn't happen with one hand, that is why, prays to

"Shani Dev", for leaving him, because even other "Devi Devta" would be witnessing, that how he has been molested and robbed, how he has been disturbed by, his employees and other relatives. What's his fault? Sieve curses the winnowing basket which in itself has seventy-two holes, the thief scolding the police. What's his fault? Nothing is his fault. Without reason, he has been disturbed and molested, if any girl's father doesn't marry her daughter, then, whether society can pull her father for touching his groom's feet? If not, then, what's his fault? Whether was his fault, that, his marriage held almost suppressing his all expectations, somewhere.

In any home, where having two or more daughters, second and other daughters are almost transgender, neither of "*Love*", nor of "Book". First searches the groom, then touches the sister's feet. First "*Ram*" will get "*Sita*" then only "*Laxman*" will get Urmila, sister of Mata Sita. That means, somewhere, till when "*Urmila*" doesn't touch "Sita's and Ram's" feet, till then, she can't get "*Laxman's*" feet.

Inside the coeducation system, whatever is appreciated by anyone, that is their present status only among those 50-100 children. Whatever was appreciated or discouraged, was their past only. Daily, new challenges come, and daily have to work, for our present. The future lies in the groom's feet only. His child is his future, his grandchild is his future, and his niece and nephews are his future. Work in the present, live in the present, children are the future. This is not necessary, that whoever did first in primary school, will also have good grades in secondary school, or higher education.

The majority of people are not honest with their future in the present. "Honesty is the best policy", with their children in the present, with their family in the present.

There is his teacher, Shri Manpreet Sandhu, who taught, "If you are bad, then he is your dad". That means, he always tries to motivate us that be honest about our future in the present while talking about the past, with children, considering children to be the future of us, and of the country. Children are the judge of any family. Who will decide, that, whether they feel ashamed or proud while introducing their guardian?

The child considers, farmers, to be the god of the country, because, they are, those, who create all. Teacher teaches to write, but farmer feeds all. Farmers means those, whom acting puppets can't compete. User of words, from different dictionaries can't compete. Dancing puppets can't compete. Farmers of Beguisrai, Land of Beguisrai, can grow anything, by the blessing of "Devi Bhumi". The child have his own Jungle, in Beguisrai, where lots of animals have their shelter, even have own ponds, and lakes, and have some sharing even in rivers, by the blessing of Devi Laxmi, and Devi Saraswati, and due to honesty of Ancestors. His Ancestors, didn't felt anything wrong while describing them.

Partition, is that act, which started from "Dwaparyug". By the presence of "Draupadi". Draupadi, the reason of "Mahabharata". Then became the reason for partition, among brothers, after that, "Abhimanyu" died. Because few years, ago, wherever Arjun was, there few year later, Abhimanyu reached. He was not knowing, that what to do there, as they both were those, who tricked to kill

"Drone Bharadwaj acharya", and asked "Ashwadhama" to beg. First killed father, then asked son to beg. First killed father or grandfather, then "Jenau" held, then was asked to beg. Like first Shri Yugal Kishore Singh died, then Shri Gaya Singh died, then kilo died, then the child was asked to beg, In the same way, first "Drone Bharadwaj Acharya" died, then "Ashwadhama" was asked to beg, Later "Abhimanyu" reached there, now, what? "Shirdi Sai", begged whole life, "Ashwadhama" begged whole life, after their death, charity, donation are expected on their name. Whole life, they begged, after them, other begged on their name. Whole life they begged, and after their death, they begged, whoever expected them to beg.

Wherever "Jenau" are expected by anyone, for their children, or grandchildren, they themselves should answer, they themselves should think, that, what is "Jenau"? and what is "Chumaan"? Whether, they will ever become grand guardian or not? Whether till they are alive, are their children or grandchildren any "Shuddar"? Bramha would be knowing better about "Chumaan", after all, act of "Jenau" happens due to the act of "Bramha", that means, he would be knowing better. Wherever, due to act or presence of any girl, *"Jenau"*, happens, that means, she can't be any relative, She is wretched women. Because, "Jenau", means, that before "Jenau", he was "Maa ki gaali", and after "Jenau" he was "Bhaduwa". And for making "Bhaduwa", guardian, grand guardian were killed first, then was made "Bhaduwa", then "Jenau" held, then was asked to beg.

Girl who becomes reason for disrespecting anyone, like *"Karan"* was disrespected by "Draupadi" and "Krishna". For a moment only, lets assume, that "*Karan*" is still alive, and "Abhimanyu" is still alive, then, whether "*Abhimanyu*" will have to touch "Karan's" feet or not? Whether "*Abhimanyu*" will touch "Duryodhan's" feet or not? Whether "*Abhimanyu*" will touch other's feet or not? While touching the feet, people earns blessing, some given "Long life", some given "*Happy life*", some gives "prosperous life", some gives "*Fertilized life*".

The first partition "*Draupadi*" or any girl should expect from their own brother, whether anyone heard that "Draupadi" did partition with "*Dhrishtadyumna*" anywhere? Girl have their right on at least in their grand guardian's property too. Guardians uses them, to rob students of coeducation. Like, once a girl danced in the school, in the year 2000, and the same year, founder Shri Raghunath Prasad Sharma died, and his M.L.A's chair reached to that girl's door. After few years, in 2004, she got gifted by a batchmate, family lost, MP's chair. Who was earning there? In such a labor, whether girl should have their right or not on their guardian's property, where they are used inside coeducational system for robbing batchmates, and schoolmates? Child labor is prohibited, there, coeducational system, is witnessed to be a place of robbing respect, property, and life, and playing with sentiments, using the daughter's or girl's face. What they will expect from the school's batchmates? Where they sing, "India is my Country, and all Indians are my brothers and Sisters". What do they sing? Coeducation should be declared to be the school of Kans, Shakuni, Ravan or not?

Shri Raghunath Prasad Sharma passed away on 2nd November 2000, someone was dancing, Shri Rambadan Singh passed away on 22ⁿᵈ December 2000, someone was dancing. Shri Nawal Kishore Singh passed away in 2004, someone was revolving, Singing, and Dancing, Shri Rajdev Singh passed away, Shrimati Anita Singh died, Shrimati Kajoma Singh passed away, Great-grandmother passed away, Two grandmothers passed away, Shri Yugal Kishore Singh passed away on 26th September 2016, Shri Gaya Singh passed away on 7th October 2017, Shri Sachidanand Singh passed away on 06th February 2023, and someone else tried to eat someone else virtue, someone else tried to eat his virtue, with their extraordinary suggestions, and someone was dancing.

His son, nor his wife, will have the right to his earned property, they can have the right to grand guardian's property. The wife has to earn "Vermilion" from her husband. His wife will have no right to his earned property, as she was not there when he was earning or begging, or was been disrespected, by her father or brother. Seeing guardian's property, whether friendship, love, or marriage happens, then why have any right to husband's earnings? If seeing guardian's property, everything has to occur then why expect any husband's earnings? Thinking even about a guardian's property makes them mentally retarded, the time they use in thinking about the guardian's property, or grand guardian's property, the same time could be used for earning. Grandchildren are the face of grand guardians. Beating, slapping, disrespecting anyone's grandchild, discouraging, means, beating, disrespecting grand guardian. Robbing a grandchild means robbing a grand guardian.

If, the grandchild is good, then they will keep the paper of the grand guardian's property in Elmira only.

According to that child's big father and father's elder brother, Shri Sachidanand Singh, the Condition remains as it is, as it was for ten years. That means someone stays there, after any incidence for ten years, somewhere. Time stays there, wherever, any incidence occurred for ten years, somewhere, for punishment or blessing. Shani Dev changes place every seven and a half years.

School means the place where all religion's children exchange their thoughts, their learning, and findings.

Coeducation is a dangerous place. That should be checked seriously. Because, that is a place where, "Violence, Gambling, Liquor, Gold, Prostitution" lies. Dancing and Singing is the first step towards prostitution, for seducing, for teasing, for robbing sights. And Raja Parikshit already had allowed "Kali" to live there where, "Violence, Gambling, liquor, Gold, Prostitution" lies. And inside the coeducation system, the most disciplined way of prostitution, teasing, or seducing all is dancing, and after that, singing comes. Dancing and singing is an act of playing with the eyeballs of children, and ears of children. For which even faculties award them, and robs all's sight. Fees were paid by all, and all's eyeballs were played, all's ears were played. Chair and respects were robbed. Pink revolution takes place, there only, black and white act happens there only.

> ➤ Why did Sita die around the age of 42-45? Not even seen the face of Menopause?

Maybe lots of reasons, like breast cancer, cervical cancer, blood cancer, menopause, and lots of health issues would be the reason, which are common in women and need care and attention from their families. Menopause can disrupt women's sleep, which means, they can behave like any mental character, she needs sleep, and care. She was, is that lady, who took care of her children's health, when they were children, vaccinating them, washing clothes for them, cooking for them, while cleaning the home, and living on fast in the name of religion on different occasions, like Ramnaumi, Chhath Puja, Durga Puja, other puja, while stitching sweater. They even take care of the property of their males. Marriage has no breakups. Wherever Sita died, that means, somewhere "Laxmi" died, "Sarswati" died, and Pooja over from that home. it can be considered to be, till when there is "Laxmi", in home, till then there is "Pooja" and vice versa. It is the male's responsibility, to take care of their "Laxmi, Saraswati, Pooja". Extra care is needed in those phases of time. Or could be many reasons. Like when her child "Love or Kush" reached the same age, where "Ram" given gift, there, she got confused somewhere, that now what? Whether the special chanting of "Malechh, Lafua, Kutta, Maa Ki Gaali, Suddar, Fail, Bhaduwa, Rascal" will occur or not? Or maybe it could be a flowering reaction to that special chanting.

"Love" has a breakup, whereas, marriage has no breakups, which means, "Breakup" should be considered to be an offense that should have the same punishment, which "Rape" has. What is a breakup? The act of making prostitutes to each other somewhere.

My grandfather had two daughters too. Shrimati Anita Singh, and Shrimati Kajoma Singh. One married to Shri Sanjeev Singh, and the other married to Shri Shailendra Prasad Singh.

➤ What is cancer?

Injury over Injury turns into cancer. Injury over Injury turns into stress or can be said Migraine. Migraine is like someone beating the skull, not visible to the common man, which increases with time. Somewhere with a sword, or brick, it is also like cancer. Which needs care.

Migraine is like "Stress" raised, after being molested, or won't be able to reply. If answered, if replied, the same day, stress over, migraine over, and that became peacock's leaf of Lord.

More than 90% of patients die in hospitals, because, there was no room for the patient in their homes which they constructed. And daily expenses of the hospital were not affordable for their lovely children, to whom they gave everything. Given land, education, clothes, freedom, and independence, to live anywhere. The child is from Patna, but goes to dozens of doors in Samhoo, because his grandfather, maintained his dignity somewhere in those homes. In Samhoo, whoever asked him to sit, He sat there.

Behind over 90% corruption, women are the main reason. Life partners are the main reason. Life partner using life partner for robbing brothers and sisters. For threatening brothers and sisters. For burning the blood of brothers and sisters. For playing with the sentiments of brothers and sisters. Because, in any school, the first pledge any child swore that, "India is my country, and all Indians are my brothers and sisters". Then expected bribe from whom? Threatened whom? Robbed whom? Disrespected whom? Insulted whom? Who threatened? Who robbed? Who disrespected? Who insulted? "Sieve curses the winnowing basket, which in itself has seventy-two holes". That means, a four-year, five years, juvenile-child "failed"? Where "Sieve curses the winnowing basket, which in itself has seventy-two holes", that means, only disrespected personalities will disrespect any child.

Teachers, Businessmen, Advocates, Doctors, and writers, earn even after their retirement. As, much old, teachers, businessmen, advocates, doctors, and writers are, that much their earnings will be. They are those, who never retire. "Sarswati" is their weapon, and respect is their earnings.

He proudly can say that his father doesn't issue any certificates, though, he neither checks copies nor sets questions. But his taught students are working in refineries, working in P.W.D, and working abroad too. He is not a bad person, by his nature. He can be introduced into society. Allegations are from those doors, who feels disturbed, from him, because, he is like, neither he eats, nor he allows to eat. He doesn't even increases fees. Teacher of the poor. Motivator of the poor. Son of a vegetable seller, son of labor, son of an Auto or truck driver, son of a Kirana seller, son of maybe a tea seller, son of good families who have earned their degree and are doing jobs, are engaged in different fields and sectors. But, due to staff, employees, and some extraordinary relatives, his name and, the institution's name are defamed. That is why, He knows, a little more about corruption inside education. Sometimes, word arrows are used from home only or from the guardian's side, or family's side, and students shout at institutions, colleges, or universities.

Some employees become over-smart while describing themselves inside any office, even they should be given an Identity Card, so that, students, guardians, and customers won't feel confused in any institution or office. Employees should be honest, by themselves. Chitragupt should be honest by himself. Whether Chitragupt have any right to take anyone's life? Chitragupt is only an accountant. He should be honest, with himself. Whether anywhere, "Yam Puja" happens? Chitragupt puja happens, whether anyone ever thought how "Yam Dev" felt? Why such Puja? For hiding whose mistakes? For putting a curtain on whose mistakes? If hiding anyone's mistake, then doing corruption or not? Laws are same for all, same law, for all. Leaders, Politicians, police, army, doctors, Engineers, readers, writers, beggars, and laborers, all are civilians. Civilians have the same human rights, that any prime minister or chief minister has. Even though I am a Civilian, having the same human rights. If, any student gets "FAIL" in any institution, please ask them to write a story about life inside that institution, inside that state, inside that country, what was going on, what was happening, and what was the environment? And sell it, in a country, where below 1% of people have the capability of writing any story in over 100 pages. And leaves them, to wait, who failed them, and expected them to come again and to pay again. The child who failed, will come, wait for a year, or two years, or even more. Bargaining is the customer's right. The child who expects grace does bargaining only.

Once Birbal reached the assembly of Raja Akbar, their, employee, or guard, expected half-sharing from the reward from Raja Akbar. Birbal expected 100 hunters on his body. Raja Akbar asked why you expected such a reward. Birbal replied, that your guard expected half sharing, that is why, he needs only 100 hunters. After that, all 100 hunters were used over that guard. Corruption is that disturbance, kept on the head. Which is also termed as "Pressure from the upper". Which is actually, pressure from the "luxurious door". The person, who will be having extra marital life, that person will be corrupt. The wife knows the "Salary" the children know the salary, the family knows the salary, but, the extra burden doesn't know the amount. Wherever the wife will be corrupt, her husband's will always feel disturbance. She only knows, that he has the source of income, and she becomes a "black cat", who tries to eat, his earnings. Honest people will never hesitate to tell the truth to anyone. Like someone kept a gun on his head using a girl, whoever was to touch his feet kept "Guns" on his head. Whether he hesitated? Girls are considered to be innocent in any situation, but that is a false statement. The girl herself is considered to be a cow, and everyone knows, that cows have no brains. They even eat plastics, which affects their health. In the same way, the girl always works on someone else suggestion or direction. They don't have their brain. They are those things. Neither family is their own, in whichever home, they take birth, nor, have any independence of even having any "Love", before marriage. Because, inside the marriage act, until and unless the girl's father doesn't touch the feet of his groom, marriage doesn't complete. That means, girls are those "Devi" who need care and love in their home only, as they are an illusion, suppose I am a girl's father, asking his daughter to dance in school, that means using the daughter's face for robbing the school, specially coeducational system. They are those, whose sacrifices can't be ignored in any aspect. They care about their brother, they care about their father, they care for their husbands, they care about their children. They have their sentiments with the "Land" where they were birth. They like to have regular family meetings, their anger means, they care about them. But, some girl, are turned that's why, they become wretched for all, as are in pain, and that is why will be found abusing and will be found cursing, and if blessing has their effect, then cursing will have their defects or not? Turned means, that if a tortoise is turned, then they die and have a life of even more than 100 years. They will become fit and fine when will are cared. Somewhere, fool people expect their death. As no one dies ever. Tortoises have a life of over 100 years and even can handle the weight of elephants, but die if are turned. They can't turn back, until and unless someone turns them back or makes them straight. It's a prayer, that, if anywhere, anyone witnesses any tortoise turned back, by any act, then, please make them straight. They will give blessing only. Their family will give blessing only. They are those things. Maybe possible that someone intentionally turned them.

Corrupt people will be found doing corruption only, corruption means a lot. Corrupt means a lot. Those who never learned "Honesty is the best policy", will be found doing corruption only.

The child visited four educational centers. Three were coeducational. The same boy achieved third division, or failed inside coeducation, and achieved first division inside the boy's educational system. Inside the boy's educational system, girls or faces of Sarswati were not serving the special numbers.

A non-teaching staff asked a student, whether uses tobacco. Whether his palm said, that uses tobacco? A teacher expected a bottle of liquor from students, A girl was told, seeing her from top to bottom, that she would never have a boyfriend by teaching faculty, inside the education system, Written complaints should be made compulsory from even children, and their guardians inside educational centers. On oral complaints, anyone can be punished? Wherever, on oral complaint, actions are taken, then, that is not any complaint. Toppers not knowing to write even any complaints. At least, in school, that should be made compulsory. On oral complaint, which action did anyone take? Who takes action on oral communication? Because actions are permanent things, whereas, oral communication is not on record. Writing communication gives schools, and colleges to use those writing expectations as any proof for the future. Oral communication means, the discussion between two people, and punishing the particular, or can be said robbing the particular. The contractor hired a person and paid, that is oral communication, whereas, writing communication means, that communication, which will be using readers even after the writer.

In a college, having more than fifty staff, including teaching and non-teaching staff, examinations held. More than four hundred students appeared in the examination. Around more than a hundred students were given a "year back", and more than three hundred students earned "First Attempt in Learning", Students protested against the result. After the protest, all students passed, and on five students management has done case or FIR, fifty staff were doing what during the protest? How, after the protest, did more than a hundred students pass, or did their year get saved? How? Whether protest was necessary to save the year of over a hundred students? Whether protest was necessary to save more than a hundred Mr. Bamula's or not?

A child given examination passed the examination from the institution, and then, expected his mark sheet and certificate, through eight written applications. After getting all service charges, and all fees paid, the institution expected children to expect marksheets and certificates by themselves from the university. Which service are they given? Even application is a protest.

Any institution's ranking increases, with healthy relations with students. Because students are the customers, and customers are the biggest advertisers of any institution or product. Teachers are sculptures of children, considering them to be the future for the country. They gives their services. What is case? Whatever the Story or act was, is and will be alive, through written communication, that is called Case.

What those fifty teaching and non-teaching faculties were doing during the protest? Five against fifty? Fifty were doing what? Whether those fifty teaching and non-teaching staff were blessing the protest? Where provoking the protest? Where doing what? More than a hundred students failed. Which service they given, that more than a hundred students earned "Year back"?

Children, who never go to school, college, or university are the safest and are more successful. Emperor Akbar was not knowing to even write an application. Shri Narendra Modi, himself has said, that he never went to school. Dr. Avul Pakir Jainulabdeen Abdul Kalam Azad studied under street lights. That means, somewhere, something is wrong in the educational system. The education system is not for hurting anyone's child. In the old days, girls were not supposed to even read and write, later they started teaching too.

Colleges, universities, schools, and institutions, all have to keep, the student's written answer sheet for a minimum of seven years in record, in file. That also comes in their services. Whether "Bhagat Singh's" file is still there or not? Whether General Dyer's file is still there or not? Whether "Nathu Ram Godsey's" file is still there or not? Then, whether student's answer sheet should be there or not? Where students are awarded "FAIL", for abusing them, using their nearby person's mouth, which means playing with the nearby person's mouth, and eyes, and playing with the ear of children. Where Mr. Bamula did suicide after having "FAIL" on a piece of paper, there, whether students' answer sheets should be kept in record, in a file for at least "Seven years" or not? So, that, more than those 75% people would become judges, who don't even know to write any application, that whether the child, who did suicide was any "Failure"?

Lots of talk happens, over the "red light" culture of VVIPs. But, "red light" should be banned inside the education system, in all aspects. As, somewhere, examiners even take open-book tests, where time remains fixed. What is red light culture? Till when, there will be dancing puppets, inside the educational system, especially inside the coeducational system, and till then, there will be a "Red light" culture.

The law allows only human rights. Humans are not supposed to hurt any animal too. Humans are also animals, animals are animals in the eyes of trees, and both are animals. Human have human rights, animal have their rights too. Even they praise god. They are the most sentimentally attached life with their loved ones. The child had a puppy, named "Kilo", who was his real well-wisher. Who realized him, that, they take every curse over them. Till then, was having "Kilo", at home, and at least no one robbed his "Key, or other properties". Kilo was a real well-wisher for him.

There is a term labor, Elephants are usually termed as labor. The child's family is full of labor, or elephant, one uncle Shri Tripurari Singh is a master in arranging labor for different private or government companies. One uncle Shri Murari Singh is an officer of Labor in the Steel Authority of India. His grandmother's younger brother, the brother-in-law of his grandfather, was Labor union president, Shri Gaya Singh. And Elephant are those things, with whom, no one fights. Elephant's brain is the biggest brain on earth, after the whale. Elephant never attacks anyone. Whether ever anyone heard or seen, that anywhere, any elephant disturbed any fruit seller? They are the most disciplined animal by nature. Elephants are herbivorous only. That is why, they are liked by all animals somewhere.

There is his other uncle, Shri Bhopal Singh, who is a farmer, groomed or trained by grand guardian's. The farmer works, then only the country eats. It is the land, that feeds all, farmers are the biggest elephant of that land.

Employees are better than relatives. Hired based on degree. Education means grooming. Grooming means officially trained in those fields or sectors. Grooming means, education. Education means grooming in that field or sector. Relatives should be banned as employees, because, that creates confusion in their children, that, whether they are relatives or employees.

Every appreciation is not an appreciation, it is just motivation, or sometimes it can be a trick of paying down some points, to provoke others to show their talent too. Inside the fair of the world, everyone is trying to pull sight of others. Whoever tried pulling the sight, is robbed the most. Oh, wow, you are so talented, Oh, wow, you are so rich, Oh, wow, you sing so well, Oh, wow, you dances so good, Oh, wow, you speak so good, Oh, wow, you are so handsome, oh, wow, you are so beautiful, oh, wow, your voice is so good. The next day, the talent of the talented person was sold, Rich person was robbed. Singers were given mikes, dancers were given dancing stages, handsome faces were sold in advertisement photos, beautiful beauties were sold on screen, and voices were sold. Topper's mark sheets were bought, by multinational companies to increase their ranking and then sell their ranking, for having investments and loans. This is the condition of appreciation.

Snakes are considered to be the most venomous animal, but, even they don't disturb humans, by themselves, without reason. They are those things. They are also a creature. Killing even a snake earns a curse. Snake has saved Vishnu, Snake has saved Krishna, Snake is also a creature, who had been found saving humans in the direction of Lord Shiva only. Snake are always found to be worshipping "Shiv Ling".

India is the country, where buyers of almost all products are available, people of India are hard working. They are working hard, in all fields and sectors. From mining to space, they are working hard. Shri Mohandas Karamchand Gandhi fought to make "Salt". Fought for Independence. Fought for their right, and fought for respect. Manufactured "Salt", then manufactured "Chandrayaan". Now, people from other countries are also working in India with respect, getting opportunities to work in India, with discipline and respect. People fight for Indian nationality, considering the country to be a better place, where, people live with unity. Some bad elements are all over, but India is a nice country. Newspapers having daily news, are printed all across the globe.

Teaching is that sector, where caste or religion doesn't matter, that is why, maybe, they are termed as "Shiksha Mafia" too from society. "Mafia" means, having no caste or religion. In his father's institute, students from all categories of families come. That means, that from all castes, gotra, and religions, the student comes. Hindus, Muslims, Christians, Sikhs, and Jains all come to have education, from them. Teachers are those things. There is his one dear friend named "Saumjit Sarkar". And he knows, one more person named "Dhankar", He knows lots of person having the name "Shiv Shankar".

According to the statement of Madam Rekha ji, a mole on her lip, was like "Nazar Battu", which means ward off evil's eye. In the same way, he considered "Mafia" as the prefix of "Shiksha" to be ward-off evil's eye, and "Shiksha Mafia" to be the blessing of god. Shri Raghunath Prasad Sharma was also called "Shiksha Mafia" inside education.

He is not, in favor of hurting any teacher. The teacher, teaches, us, the teacher teaches our children, and the teacher teaches our guardians. Teachers are those things, who feed students. Who feeds students with their words. Like, "Right now, are father's children, whenever, will become the father of children, that day, you will come to know". They took children to zoos, to parks, or somewhere on different occasions. They are those things. They are the disguised faces of the guardians. But, children are real "Guru", because, almost all teachers are living the life of after "Jenau" somewhere. And they are only an acting child somewhere. Children are the face of "Ram", the moment, "Daksha", and "Ravan" slapped or disrespected, and that "Ram" married "Parvati", the same "Ram" became "Shiv", that means, children are real "Guru", and with children, human should be honest.

Employees should be honest, and hired by seeing the acknowledgment certificate, or mark sheet from institutions, Not based on relation, Employees hired based on degree, will expect an experience certificate, but, employees hired based on relation, will expect what? They will chop knives and will run away. You can't even gossip about the fraud from relatives, will gossip about whom? To become even a smart laborer or contractor, the person should have an ITI degree. I know, two electricians, one is "Choubey ji" who gives his work to someone else, somewhere and the other is "Murli ji" who has good knowledge as an electrician.

There is a joke maker, Joker, who makes jokes over every word with their comment, which damages them only. Because no one knows, on which occasion, who will become their own and who will become what for them? Whether ever anyone from Gujrat, thought that Shri Narendra Damodar Das Moolchand Modi, son of tea seller, proclaimed "Fakir", proclaimed "Guard", would ever become prime minister of the country?

While scolding, and disrespecting, people try to break other's confidence, like oh you "FAILED", oh, you can't do this, oh, you are incapable of doing this, oh, this is not in your capability, Oh you are the son of tea seller, Oh, you are "Fakir". The moment you left, that person himself, that person's close tried that. The moment, you left, someone else from your own family, tried that. It is elders who give confidence and break confidence too, not knowing the fact, that, at last, they will have their world in their feet only. Whoever are our guardians today, they will become our children tomorrow. Whatever they will behave with their children, will earn the same as their children.

Health is wealth. Early morning walks, and early morning exercise make humans healthier, and mentally fit, which makes them wealthy too. Specially, there are lots of health issues, which are resolved with early morning walks. An early morning walk gives fresh air to the human respiratory system.

Education doesn't mean only to have any degree. A confectioner, chef, Barber, tailor, carpenter, blacksmith, sculpture, Driver,

Mechanic, Milk maker, etc, all are well educated, in their field. They take care of their work. Even drivers, and guards, take care in their work. They earn experiences, and experiences make them more educated day by day. Driver and guard are that profession, the day, when they made any mistake, that day, becomes their last day.

People, who think, that, they have achieved anything big, in their life, they fool themselves. The day, when they thought that achieved success, that day was their last day only. They haven't achieved anything. Time has given them, and time takes back, time is the most powerful and strongest among all. Time can make Beggar to be King, King to be Joker, and Joker to be beggars. Respect time, time will respect you too. Time gives everyone a chance, to perform, on the stage, of which we are puppets or variables. Wherever, we are today, someone else was ever before, and someone else will be tomorrow. There is a song, "Name will change, face will change", that means, wherever we are today, someone else was ever before, and someone else will be tomorrow.

Respect others, others will respect you. After losing anyone, people have to feel regret only.

The child mates two persons, one class topper, and the other a teacher. Asked them a question, both didn't answer the question. The class topper, said, that has forgotten and the teacher said, that we learn daily, and we read daily the same book. That means, who "FAILED" to understand? Class toppers were asked to write a letter, and all children and their guardians will read, and will try to understand, their "Hand Writing". All were given the opportunity and asked them to sit in between a hundred students, and their guardians, and was asked, and expected them to write a single-page application. Their handwriting was hardly read by anyone. Because they, themselves never wrote during the classwork or homework. Inside the education system, only discussion over any topic happens. Inside discussion, who "FAILED" and who "Passed"? "Marksheets" are decorated pieces of paper, Handwritten letters of the majority of policemen, doctors, and judges who need assistance to read, can be read hardly. How, their handwriting, was understood by those who awarded them any topper? They were those things, always having to shine "Lobbying certificates".

A patient died, in a Hospital having lots of experienced doctors, who "FAILED" in that situation? Which degree, and experience do they have in that situation? The doctor's first and last duty is to save the patient in all aspects by their services. Patient means, customer for "Doctor", the customer is the face of god, and customer died, means god died. As many customers become "Fit and Fine" that much blessings they earn from their families. Sincerity should be in their work. Abusing, disrespecting, even dead man, can make mental. A dead person's path is not obstructed. They are also the face of god.

Women intentionally do some act, on the direction of their suggestion makers, which can't be justified. Like dressings. From school, it should be taught to have "Chunari, Dupatta, Burkha", it should be taught to prefer "Salwar Suit", in the country of "*Laxmi, Saraswati, Durga, Kaali*".

Wherever girl's are used for earning, that home becomes mentally retarded. That home, becomes the home of mentally sick people, by nature. "*Laxmi*" going to earn "*Laxmi*"? And "*Sarswati*" going to have any certificate of being "Literate"? Women are the face of mothers and sisters.

Experience comes with work to be done. As, much work is done, that much experience anyone earns. Experience means that phase which anyone spent in their field or sector. Those time, they given, in that field or sector. Those works, that have been completed, in the past. Like, anyone who constructed five apartments, as a builder. That is their experience. Like someone wrote fifty or hundred novels, that is their experience. Like someone taught, lakhs of students, that is their experience. Like someone is a very good chef. Like someone sold hundreds of plots, as a broker, or land developer, then that is their experience. Like someone constructed "Dev Lok", where all "Devi Devta" got shelter in over 100 acres, that is their experience. A person, who retires from any job field, or sector, has earned lots of experience somewhere.

Beauty lies in the eyes of anyone. Wherever you watch, wherever your sight goes, that area becomes beautiful. That means beauty lies in your eyes.

Never laugh at anyone, and never make anyone cry. A differently-abled person is more stable and almost fixed to their birthplace. Cares more for all family members. A failed child does more labor than those who achieved a topper's certificate. Did top in what, where it was written to "answer in own words"? In copying? In cram or rote or to learn the same. Some students cram questions of mathematics too. Did top in abusing? They are those things.

Those who smile at others should keep patience, life will take care of them too. Never disrespect grand guardian. They are ornaments of any family. Diamonds, and gold, are not of any use, guardians are real ornaments. As much united family remains, that much of their strength remains. Whatever I know, just because of my grand guardian.

"Sieve curses the winnowing basket, which in itself has seventy-two holes", the Thief scolded the police. Oh, how much talented, topper we are, that we abused anyone? Abusing for what? The moment anyone abused, or disrespected, the same moment, all education went into drainage. Abused and became accused, that much talented and topper we are. Abused, then shown any literate culture?

Money is dirt of hand. Money is the scum of hand. Money is the face of Lizard, which changes colors.

> ➤ What is the crown, and what is the chair, what is the Coronation?

It is an illusion, created for playing with the eyeballs of viewers. Every animal has their life span. Fox can live up to 2-14 years, with the blessing of "Surya Dev". Dogs can live 10-12 years, by the blessing of "Surya Dev", Lion can live up to 10-15 years, and Crocodile's life span ranges from 25-70 years depending on the species. Elephants have a life span of 48 to 70 years, depending on the species. Hippopotamus can live 40-50 years. Tortoises can live 100-150 years or even more. Whales can live up to 100-250 years depending on their species. There what is crowning? What is coronation? What is the chair? Whale is watching every act of any family, tortoise is watching every act of any family. Human life exists after crossing all species of life. The population of life is as it is, as it was a thousand years ago. A thousand years ago, there were over millions of elephants in India, the population of elephants decreased, and humans increased. The population of life remains the same. All are spies of god, gossipers. Even house fly gossip among them, which are audible and visible to god. Tortoise witnesses, whale witnesses, all witnesses, every act around them, around us. Whether crow, vulture, Falcon, or Eagle witnessed or not, how humans are fooling humans, robbing humans. There is a song,

deep shadow of silence

Villages filled with silence

This bridge has been raised on the river

The earth is vast and vast

These fields are scorched by weeds

This empty path has been understood

This mother kills the whole world

These black smokes in this house

These black smokes in this house

Hoho..

Hmmm..

My enemies, my brothers, my enemies

My enemies, my brothers, my enemies

Because of me, we both say these things at home.

What does a destructed garden say?

Hey..

My enemies, my brothers, my enemies

Hoho...

Hmmm..

The body became heavier than the blood.

This is the sun of death, this is the rising wind.

There are two brothers, who even after having partition fought, for more, one tried to capture the other's rights or property, even after partition. That is why, guardians are necessary, even after partition, for maintaining peace, inside the family. Guardian means, in whose feet, all work was going. The biggest sensor lies in the guardian. Who did what, in whose presence, and in whose direction, on whose "word arrow" guardian knows all? For Ram, a child, there is no boundary, no partition, he always has his "Crown", with him. Even after partition, he goes anywhere.

Arrogance always pulls towards begging. Arrogance means someone will curse. Arrogance means will earn a curse from somewhere.

The term working women is associated with Lazy women, who don't work at home, run from work of home, and say that are working women. The child's mother, the child's grandmother, did that much work, that no working lady did. Mother means, homemaker. In the home, they have so much work, that, they have no time to go for any job. They use their time at home only. Home knows them only. Housewife, means, that the wife, who lives at home only, like any goddess lives at any particular place. In 24 hours a day, after having sleeping hours, and after having teeth brushed, bathing, and worshipping, how many hours does anyone have? At the same time, did worked at home and worked other places too. Have any time left for children? Have time for a guardian? Have any time for the home where they got married?

Wherever partition happens, the women of the house feel most hurt. Because they feel, that, now will niece or nephew's ever come? Now, niece or nephew's child will ever come? Guardian feels most hurt when partition happens. Considering their children to be worthless, they expected partition in the direction of "Draupadi and Dhrishtadyumna". He used to go to his grandfather's brother's, Shri Nawal Kishore Singh's home too, to meet grandmothers, even after the partition. Why do girls expect partition, when they are the face of "Laxmi"? Why?

"Do the work, don't think about the result, work is worship, work is offerings too".

The matter of smile is that, for writing a novel, creating a novel, manufacturing a novel, or doing "*Mann Ki Baat*" on paper, there is no need for any permission or affiliation. But, the school, and college, need permission or affiliation for facilitating children and students to learn to read and write. Permission or affiliation!!! However, hospitals need permission to do the treatment of patients. For establishing a company, school, college, or hospital, permission is needed, by those who achieved good grades in their examination. Permission and affiliation are just a trick for bribes only. Which needs to be blessed, and in the words of Shri Lalit Ghoswami, punishment means blessing.

➤ What is good grades?

In "**Mahabharata**", "*Duryodhan*" was having "*Narayani Sena*" of "*Krishna*". In **Ramayana**, "*Shani Dev*" himself decorated the life of "*Ravan's*" children. But, all his children failed to gain a "Long life" from "*Shani Dev*", because, they never learned to bow down. Shani Dev, can decorate the environment, can decorate the home, can decorate the "Marksheet and certificates", and can decorate health, but can't teach anyone to touch their feet for even have a "Long life". What is "Good grades"? And what is permission or affiliation from those having good grades or can be said from "Duryodhan"?

Time never goes anywhere. Suppose the child is the "Sun" and sees all revolving around him. he is fixed, all planets, with their moon, revolving around him. From his Shine, all are Shining, and showing their moons. Where even their moon is shining from his shine only. All planet and their home are shining from his Shine only. For him, all are revolving around him. It is they, who are revolving in a particular orbit. It is they, who are moving, it is they, who are completing a revolution at a particular time. But they are not supposed to touch his feet. They can only revolve around him. For thousands, or more than a thousand years, they will only revolve, but, can't touch his feet like any "Dancing puppet" at any party. They are those things. For him, time is stopped, as he is fixed, even after thousands of years, he will be there only, but for someone, time is running.

The sun never goes anywhere, the sun remains fixed. Earth rotates. Hole in a cloud, the shadow of the earth changes the shape of the moon.

The affiliation process should be easier, the registration process should be easier, permitting process should be easier. The child is not in favor of so lengthy process, where at every stage, bribes are expected. In the words of Shri Manmohan Singh, Money doesn't grow on a tree. Bribe for what? As, much online registration, and online submission, that much honest system will be. Online submission, means, visible to all. Like our home assignments were asked to submit in online, in Post graduation. During COVID-19, schools, and colleges facilitated children and teachers to study and to teach from home.

Suppose, He established a college or university. At every step, whether have to give a bribe? Then will ask for what? Whether ever will ask for any permission? Will teach what? Whether He is mentally ill, who went to ask, can he establish a college or university or any company in the country that gained independence in 1947? Independence of what? Of taking permission? Whether, for being affiliated, for establishing a college or university, or any company, whether anyone need any permission? Whether child ask his mother before peeing or doing porty? In which environment people have to ask, can establish a school, college, university, or any company? That would be better, that will beg or protest out of those agency's office, who allots permission. They can't disrespect even a beggar, they have no right, because suppose someone is begging, then in that, anyone has any problem? It is a very nice trick. Because if will disrespect even a beggar, will earn a curse. Will lose them, whoever was in their feet, or in whoever feet they were while abusing and cursing. Begging is also a way of protest.

While constructing a college, labor got jobs, after constructing a college, teachers got jobs while running a college, management, teacher, and all will be found paying taxes, then bribe for what? Whether the premise of "Sarswati", whether premise of Lord Bramha, and Whether premise of Lord Shiva, whether that premise will give a bribe, which teaches "Honesty is the Best Policy"? How anyone can expect a bribe? The bribe is also like extortion. If anyone paid tax, then for what he paid tax? If has to bribe, if has to give extortion, then why tax? Either take the bribe or take the tax or take extortion. More than fifty country knows the language "English". Either use "I love you" phrase, or use the book door to door. Lots of temples' main priests are "SC/ST". Political pandit, the term, in itself, is a term, which says a lot.

The child, as Brahman Bharadwaj Bhumihaar, says, that, the festival, having no presence of "Brahman", that festival is called "Chhath Mahaparv". Ramayana is that "Holy Book" which should be read during marriage only, not every year. Because, it is a book, knowing "Marriage Act", where "Vibhishan" touched the feet of "Ram" and completed the marriage. Every month, which salary? Whose marriage occurring every year? No one can take the place of that act, and even the father-in-law even has to touch his groom's feet. Read a hundred times, same book, and nothing will change. Wherever "Pandit" and "Jajman" act happens, that means, sometimes, police will be used, sometimes, someone else will be used, sometimes school will be used, sometimes, criminals will be used, and "Jajman" will be found paying interest on interest. Because, "Jajman" was not knowing, that, someone else was using the girl's face to rob the school, office, and institution, and the girl's mother was answering using the girl's face. "Jajman" did not know, that, from the one hand, "I Love You" phrase was provoked, and on the other hand "Book" were expected. Why child goes to school? Why do any guardian send their children to school? For checking what? For checking the "I love you" phrase? Or for learning reading and writing? For making *"Sati"*, lord Shiva was not responsible.

For establishing an automobile company, permission is needed? For establishing a company, that will offer millions of jobs, where rotation of trillions of crores will take place, permission is needed? A car mechanic established a garage and gave jobs to dozens. What is permission? What is affiliation? These are tricks for bribes. The government's employees are "Beggars", with whom, if will talk, they will become "Beggars". As, Shri Narendra Damodar Das Moolchand Modi, already had declared himself to be "Fakir", then whether his employees are "Fakir's" employees or not?

The day, when the opposition will become honest, that day, the country will develop. Corrupt opposition always remains silent, because their whole file is with the ruling party.

Suppose, in the governance of Shri Narendra Damodar Das Moolchand Modi, India did expense of around Rupees eight thousand crores, in changing the color of notes. Within five years, did anyone see where those pink revolutionary notes were disposed? On what, those Rupees eight thousand crores were spent? Did expense of over four lakh crores over-vaccination during COVID-19, but nowhere mask of rupees five were distributed for free. Where, viruses can't be created nor be destroyed, as per the words from the book of Biology, of class 9th, 10th. Constructed Prabhu Shri Ram's temple, where Ram was in their own family. Plays with eyeballs and sentiments of civilians and citizens, using different media and channels. Does that mean the whole work is zero somewhere or not?

Education means, making an honest personality. Honesty should be in themselves. "If the child is good, then why to accumulate wealth, if the child is bad, then why to accumulate wealth"?

By himself, he might be honest, as like the character of the movie "Gopi Kishan" of "Suresh Oberoi", Shri Narendra Damodar Das Moolchand Modi, may would be surrounded by robbers only. But, He once used a line, "In the bathroom, someone was taking shower wearing a raincoat", which suits him too.

He had committed that he never go to school, and never had learned to write any application.

Shri Damodar Das Moolchand Modi would be watching, as no one dies ever. Shri Mohandas Karamchand Gandhi is still on the globe, Pandit Jawaharlal Nehru is Still on the Globe, Md Firoz Khan is still on the globe, Shri Rajeev Gandhi is still on the globe, Shri Sanjay Gandhi is still on the globe, Shri Atal Bihari Vajpayee is still on the globe. Shri Rajesh Khanna is still on the globe, Dr. Shri M.G.R is still on the globe, and Shri Subbarao is still on the globe. Shri Bala Saheb Thackeray is still on the globe.

Whoever sown the seed of corruption, and extortion, from where they will eat the fruit of honesty? Corruption kills own children. Corruption earns a curse from others. Wherever there will be corruption, that means, whatever is in their feet, that is corruption. Copying with others fools themselves. Copying someone else. Income "Fifty paise, and expense in Rupees". That means, Copying damages own. Copying damages own property, life, and time. If the child starts copying the life of Ambani, or Bill Gates, or Larry Elison, or Eion Musk, or Charley Rolls, or Henry Royce, then will fall or not?

The child is not here to copy anyone's life. He doesn't support copying anyone. Every person has their own personality, and way of life, and does their own "Mann Ki Baat" or "answers in their own words".

Manufacturers, and developers, all are those things, who create jobs, and pay taxes too. Not only taxes, but creates a system, where their employees even pay taxes. That means they should be preferred more.

Laptop manufacturing companies, Automobile companies, Schools, colleges, Hospitals, ICD, CFS, construction companies, Film stars, Film directors, theater owners, all companies under ITC, all companies of HUL, Paint companies, Cement companies, Airline companies, telecom company, transportation companies, Dairy companies, utensils companies, chemical companies, FMCG companies, farmers, contractors, builders, Government employees pays taxes, all pays taxes, their employees pays taxes. If they all are paying taxes, then for what they are paying? They expect a corruption-free state, a corruption-free country. They pay, for crime-free, for their safety, and a respectful life, in all aspects.

Shri Narendra Damodar Das Moolchand Modi, said on ease of business, Which, business? For establishing a "Salt company" Shri Mohandas Karamchand Gandhi, did protest. Whether for establishing any school, college, institution, university, cement company, Paint company, ICD, CFS, Laptop company, refrigerator company, automobile company, E-commerce company, management needs to protest or to pay "bribe"? In such system people migrates. Businessman migrates. Leaving them to live hungry. And to fight among themselves, rob each other, fight with each other, crime increases with decrease in number of Businessman's. Crime decreases, when number of businessman's increases. Because they establishes a system where rotation of money, generation of revenue takes place. Which reduces poverty. They are those things. Hurting a single businessman, kills lots of jobs. Unemployment increases from wherever businessman migrates.

Every day is new, every day have to face new challenges. Every day, new customer comes. Marksheet, experience certificate, all are their past only, seeing which, anyone expects them to work in present, as per their certificate presented at anywhere, for getting an experience certificate in future, and that future will be their present someday, for further future, that means, present is past of future.

> ➤ Who is poor and who is rich?

A person having 1000 acre land in Chennai is rich inside Chennai, A person having 500 Acre land in Mumbai is richer than him, A person having 400 Acre land in New Delhi, is richer than they both, a person having 100 acre land in London is richer than they all three. A person having 50 acres in Dubai, is richer than all four, depending on locality. Who is richer and who is poor? Someone has great resources of water, someone has great resources of Petroleum product, someone has great resources of Marble, someone has great resources of coal, someone has great resources of Diamond, someone has great resources of Aluminium, Someone has great resources of copper, someone has great resources of Iron, someone has great resources of magnesium, someone has great resources of Diatomite, someone has great resources of eatables, someone has great resources of Rohu fish, someone has great resources of Tuna fish. If the customer is expecting "water", then will serve a "cold drink or tea"? What that customer will do?

Today, transportation has become much easier. From India, people are importing Tuna Fish, Rohu Fish, other fishes, Sereal, Pulses, Rice, wheat, Coffee, Jaggery, medicines, metals, timber, fruits, and other natural products.

The payment system has become much easier. Letter of credit, Demand Drafts, RTGS, NEFT, and Bank are becoming guarantors. Banks have given opportunities for businesses to grow. Banks are also doing business by giving their services. Banks are selling gold bonds too, which are also used as a payment method.

Some investors are buying plots, and giving them to developers or builders to develop the land, for making complexes, apartments, and colonies. They all are contributing to the system.

Even after studying became a Donkey, even after studying doing "Debt slavery". Those who expect to give in writing, from "Writers", so that, they would ever become like them, can't become like them ever. Copying for what? Copier copies some words from here and lived past according to somewhere else. That means made some mistakes in the past and then copied some mistakes from here in the present. If copying anyone, then copy them only. Because "laundry's dog is neither of home nor of Ghat". Copy only guardian's.

Suppose, A manufacturer, manufactured a product of MRP Rs 100. Paid GST 28%, then shopkeeper's profit of around 10%, then distributor's margin, of around 10%, then transportation cost, then, packaging, electricity bill, staff payment, office expense, advertisement expense. What was the real cost of that product, for which the customer paid Rs 100? What was the real manufacturing cost? Whether the real cost of that product was below thirty or twenty or not?

If suppose, A person threatened anyone's family, in the country, where It is taught, "India is my country, and all Indians are my brothers and sisters", they threatened whom? They extorted whom? There who robbed whom? There who abused whom? Whether threatened, extorted, robbed, brothers and sisters or not?

Either a human is in someone's feet, or someone else will be in their feet. If shown anger, if cursed anyone, then cursed whom? Either, them, whoever were their feet, or in whoever feet they were. Lost whom? Either, in their feet, or in whos ever feet they were or not? Anger is the seed of destruction. And to make angry, people provoke, abuses, and disrespect somewhere.

The child does not support the coeducation system. The coeducation system means corruption from top to bottom. Disguise faces of family members will be found to disturb children, from getting leave from their responsibilities. Robbed girls are used for robbing batchmates. After school hours, what do they do? Where do they go? Coeducation is the place where Surpankha lies.

If any boy was expected to give in writing, that has been called "Malechh, Lafua, Shuddar, Mental, Kutta, Maa ki gaali, Bhaduwa, Rascal, Beggar, Fail", as any complaint, then can understand, that how much talented they would be. Where Mr. Bamula did suicide after having "Fail" on a piece of paper. That means, someone intentionally tried to kill someone, or someone intentionally tried to provoke to suicide, or someone used his nearby person to abuse him, that your child failed, or to give in writing, that has been said "Malechh, Lafua, Shuddar, Mental, Kutta, Maa ki Gaali, Bhaduwa, Rascal, Beggar, Fail", or someone tried to change the place of someone with child. For example, Whether Shri Narendra Damodar Das Moolchand Modi is any child? Who never went to school? Who tried to fool whom? Whether no one taught him to maintain "Pin drop silence"? Worshipped of killing someone, by their abusing, and complaining act.

Inside "Mahabharata", "Duryodhan" was asked by "Gandhaari" to meet her in the morning without clothes, so that, she can make his body of stone, Where, "Krishna" tricked, and asks him to have something to hide those body parts, where beating was not allowed. What "Krishna" will say, over followers of the "Jain" religion? What "Krishna" will say, to any girl's father, who uses, their girl's face for abusing, considering girls to be only an illusion? Like, in someone's eyes "Bhaduwa" is good, because they easily can use "I love you" phrase, in someone's eyes before becoming "Bhaduwa" they are "Maa ki Gaali", in someone's eyes, if working and sweating then looking "Malechh, Shuddar", and if taken four times bath, then looking "Bhaduwa" not looking groom, he is looking "Bhaduwa". Because girl are nothing inside the marriage act, they are only teasing machines. Beauty and dirt all lie in eyes only. Indian women's culture. Indian women's extraordinary "Draupadi's/Sati/Sita/Ravan" behavior after getting fed. After getting gifted. Girls are Snakes by nature. As, they are only an illusion, or puppet. Singing and dancing both occur in the same chess cube, and inside the marriage girl's father even has to touch their feet, and then the marriage completes. There, what they are?

In the same way, if the girl didn't take a bath, then are "maid", and if taken a bath, and used "Lipstick", then looking prostitute or not? As every action has an equal and opposite reaction. While abusing "Sieve curses the winnowing basket, which in itself has seventy-two holes". If any girl's father or brother, says "Maa ki Gaali" to any child, then which Gaali they are? Beti ke gaali, Bahin ke gaali? If any girl says "Bhaduwa", what she is? "Love" is always provoked by girl. "Mahabharata" is also provoked by girl.

There is a chanting prayer

> "Om Bhur Bhuvassuvaha |
> Tatsa Viturvarenyam |
> Bhargo Devasya Dhimahi |
> Dhiyo Yonaha Prachidayat || Swaha".

There is another chanting prayer *"Aarti Kunj Bihari Ki Shri Girdhar Krishna Murari Ki"*, and there is special chanting by "Political Pandit's" groups, for saving their extraordinary post of getting salaried every month, that "Malechh, Lafua, Kutta, Maa Ki Gaali, Shuddar, Bhaduwa, Fail, Rascal". "Surya Putra Karan" was said, "Shudder". Because some children are of Surya dev only, and due to them, those extraordinary people abuse. "Surya Putra Karan's" shield was robbed, and then he was killed, using his brothers somewhere. Girls themselves are the biggest "Suddar", by birth, they are "Beghar". "Sita" was found thrown in "Sitamarhi". When it is considered "Sita" to be top class, who was by birth a "Beghar", there, what are "Fakir's employee's daughter's or sister's"?

This is the situation of the "Coeducation system". The girl's father uses a towel or daughter, to rob the bull's earnings. For disrespecting Bull. Shared his own experience. The girl is like this towel, illusion only. In last, that bull will become "Joker", "Beggar" or "Vanvaasi". Like, after getting the ring from "Ram", "Ram" looked "Vanvaasi, Fakir, Beggar". This is the condition of "Sita" and "Ram", this is the condition "Devki" and "Vasudev", this is the condition of "Kans" and "Vasudev". This is the condition of "Ram" and "Ravan".

The day, when, this bull, changed the target towards that ringmaster, or joker of the stadium, that day, this bull won. Bull is god, for that ringmaster or joker, if that bull stopped acting, then, the whole system ends. But, due to the nature of the bull, in over a dozen bulls, this ringmaster or joker remains safe. Who is god in this situation for all? And the moon of lord shiva is like that red towel, even if that "Joker" leaves this towel for that bull, then also, it will damage that bull only. That means coeducation is a dangerous place. that will damage that bull's head, in all aspects. This is the condition of coeducation. Does this joker have any capability of even touching that bull? This is "Ravan", who uses "Sita" and "Sita" uses him, for robbing "Ram".

Girl father and brother spoil time of own, and children too, this is the condition of the "Coeducation System". Shared his feedback, shared his experience. Whether on the direction of this joker, can great grandson of Shri Rambadan Singh be punished? Whether on the direction of this joker, can grandson of Shri Yugal Kishore Singh be punished? Whether on the direction of this joker, can grandson of Shri Nawal Kishore Singh be punished? Whether on the direction of this joker, can grandson of Aja be punished? Where they themselves were teaching that "India is my country and all Indians are brothers and sister", there who made "Sati"?

"Surya Dev" would be knowing, that, how inside the coeducational system, children are robbed. "Sataisa" children are robbed. Those who haven't opened their eyes yet, are robbed. Someone robbed eyes, someone robbed "Shield", someone robbed "Navel", using girl. "Surya Dev" would know, the treatment too. School is not any marriage bureau.

It is a bitter truth, that, due to "Chhathi's children", "Sataisa" children have to suffer. "Chhathhi" children, delays in every act, and eats "Sataisa's" children's time and rights. For example, If, anywhere, the elder son, married after 30, then till that, what "Bharat, Laxman, Shatrughan" should do? Where the government of India says, that boys should be married after 21, and girls should be married after 18, there, what do they do while posing, while delaying? What do they do? Respecting doesn't mean, that, anyone gets the right to abuse. Abusing for what? "Sataisa" children were looking "Malechh", whether he was to become groom? Whether he was to use perfume or powder? Whether he was to be shot in any photo? Ram was the elder brother of "Bharat", which means, on his head, "Ram's" wooden slipper or "Khadau" was kept. "Khadau" of "Ram", on the head of "Bharat".

The child swears, that he will never send his child in a coeducational system. It is a factory for making beggars. It is a factory for making "Prostitute and Bhaduwa". It is a factory of killing grand guardians, it is a factory of killing guardians, it is that factory, where the girl's father, becomes the suggestion maker, and then the girl's brother becomes the suggestion maker. After complaining about anyone, can anyone expect any "I love you" phrase? It is a factory of "Mahabharata" only. Tutankhamun, married his own cousin's sister, which means, earlier father was teasing and suggesting, and then his brother teased him. The ruler of 7 Gotra, Kans, became King, and the ruler of 11 Gotra was imprisoned. The child swears, that he will never send his child to a coeducational system. It is a Garbage system. Used for making transgender. The girl will sit ahead, will start robbing, will start robbing sights, will start teasing, will start provoking, and the girl's father, and mother, will plan the next day's activity for that school's environment. If the girl's father slaps her, then will do what? In whichever home, a girl takes birth, that home should not be provocative. If the girl provokes someone else with the phrase "I love you" then will do what? What is "Mahabharata"?

MLA, MP's chair are stolen from someone's door, guardian died, other family member died, slapped, beaten, abused, whether the system is the system of making "Transgender" or not?

If suppose, any child "Failed" and established a school, college, or company, like others did. and inside the MBA program, taught by faculties, that inside the business, even needs to abuse too, and hired a person having any nice degree, then whether that employee will abuse the owner? Or owner will? Who will ask questions in that company? The owner will or not? The day, when the employee abused, the same day, they will be terminated from their job, and that will become their experience certificate, or can be said, that, they left their job somewhere. They are toppers in their past, in their college in someone's eyes, but are laborers wherever they will be hired. The boss is always right, there it doesn't matter, that which degree he or she has. M.D.H Masala company's owner, Mahashay Dharmpal Gulati, doesn't have any degree. Shri Narendra Damodar Das Moolchand Modi, himself has declared that he never went to school. Emperor Akbar doesn't even know how to write an application. Charles Babbage, assignment was not shown to anyone, ever. Bill Gates, Mark Zuckerberg, Steve Jobs, Larry Ellison, and many more are college dropouts. Because they felt something wrong. Whatever others said was right, and whatever they said was wrong? For reading the majority of class topper's handwriting, assistance will be needed. Because they never did homework by themselves, their guardian did. For making handwriting, more than two and a half K.G. pressure is needed, there who failed and who passed? And school, decorated their Marksheets, for playing with the eyeballs of owners or for playing with the ears of owners through the mouth of managers, or secretaries, or surroundings. Doctors did top, but their handwriting is hardly read by any patients or their relatives, but they are doctors.

Employees of any company should have some distance from their owners. Owners should have some distance from their employees, in any business. Otherwise, they trick a lot—specially relatives. Inside jobs, there are no "Sentiments". The child has picked those packets, for whom, the employee expects laborers. For any boss, employees are also labor. Employees can have four promotions in their life in the government sector, first after seven years of joining, second after twelve years of joining, third after twenty years of joining, and fourth after twenty-five years of joining, seeing all previous records.

After every disrespect, people give others the right to disrespect them too or provoke others to answer in their own words.

➢ What is writing?

The skill, that maintains the Pin-drop silence, and establishes communication using pen and paper only, is called writing. In writing communication, overwriting is not allowed. Wherever over-writing happens, wherever pen over pen is used over writing communication, that means, "Police is a thief". Police mean, maternal uncle too, in the words of "Munna Bhai MBBS". And Pen means a lot and paper means a lot too.

Writing means the skill that is used for communicating with even those, who died, considering, that no one dies ever, wherever, we are today, someone else was ever before, and someone else will be tomorrow. I feel, that, Shri Yugal Kishore Singh, Shri Rambadan Singh, Shri Gaya Singh, Shri Nawal Kishore Singh, Shrimati Anita Singh, and Shrimati Kajoma Singh, are still reading, whatever the writer wrote.

One remembers by writing, the writer also remembers by writing. It is taught in school, remember by writing.

Writers are also labor. For example, he wrote, "India is Great, Bharat is Great". That means did labor. Lots of 25, 50, 75, 100-year children can't write. They can feel easy to pick bags or weigh of over 100 K.G, but can't write any "Line, or application". That means children go to school, to be groomed to become writers. Takes training to become a writer. The writer has no age. A child of 14, 16, 18, 20, or 25, wrote an application, where, application, means, that weapon, which is used for using surrounding, using themselves for gossiping among themselves. That means child of 14, 16, 18, 20, and 25 used a weapon, learnt from the door of "Bramha, Vishnu, Mahesh". Provoked from the door of "Saraswati, Laxmi, Parvati". Whoever is groomed or trained in whichever field or sector, becomes more experienced day by day.

It is not necessary, that only printed applications will have value, Prem Behari Narain Raizada, hand-wrote an application that became law. Actually writing and reading is law, human have human rights only.

"Saraswati is the face of Laxmi, Laxmi is the face of Parvati, Parvati is the face of Sarswati", that means, on the one hand, they expect "I love you" phrases, and on the other hand they expect writers to give in writing. Spoiler of their own home. Not any homemaker, they can be said home burners.

Coeducation is the worst place, neither marriage happens, nor love happens, it is the place of making "Sati" only.

If any education system is worst or garbage, then because of their students. A child who "Failed" is worst in the eyes of good? Who made them good and who made them bad? If any school, college is worst, then, that how, toppers are good? If any child is worst, in any education system, according to toppers, according to healthy, wealthy peoples, having "Narayani Sena" and if "Sieve curses the winnowing basket, which in itself has seventy-two holes", "Thief scolding the police", then what they are? But coeducation is always a doubtful and confusing place.

➤ Why writing is above speaking?

Writing is above speaking, because, he wrote, he prayed, for the wellness of Ram, which means, he used even readers for the same prayer, for the wellness of Ram. He prayed, for a corruption-free Country, which means, He even used, the readers for the same, for doing the prayer, where they even prayed for a corruption-free country. He prayed, whoever founds showing eyes to Bharat, Hindustan, India, whoever founds disrespecting Bharat, Hindustan, India, they become blind, their hands got chopped, their legs got chopped, their tongue got chopped, they become landless, they become powerless, speechless, Navel less that means, He used readers for doing the same prayer, that whoever founds showing eyes to Bharat, Hindustan, India, whoever founds disrespecting Bharat, Hindustan, India, they become blind, their hands got chopped, their legs got chopped, their tongue got chopped, they become landless, they become powerless, speechless, Navel less. Written book or applications, is a set of worship, that come alive, whenever anyone reads those applications or books, through the reader's mouth.

When I wrote,

Pakistan (P)	Bhukha (B)	Pyasa(P)
Hindustan (H)	Hara (H)	Bhara (B)

Then I prayed,

Pakistan (P)	Bhukha (B)	Pyasa(P)
Hindustan (H)	Hara (H)	Bhara (B)

And used the readers to pray the same prayer,

Pakistan (P)	Bhukha (B)	Pyasa(P)
Hindustan (H)	Hara (H)	Bhara (B)

It is taught, to teach girls, to save girls, because somewhere, they are the most illiterate personalities. They are the illusionary faces of their father and brothers used for robbing only. The girl's father touched his head, which did "Kanya Daan" on his head, The girl father's needs education, not girls. Blessing lies in the feet of the groom. Not on the head of the groom. And girls are themselves illusion, blessing rights change place. Whoever saw the face of Krishna in Mahabharata, lost the battle, whoever took shelter in the feet of Krishna, won the battle. Arjun touched the feet of Krishna, then later Krishna even touched his feet, and married his sister with "Arjun". Inside marriage, the Groom touches the feet of the father-in-law, and the father-in-law has to touch the feet of his groom.

Once Shri Pandit Jawaharlal Nehru went to England for higher studies. There he mate Md Ali Jinnah. Both mate a girl, or can be said, that the same girl was fooling both. Like Rahu and Ketu were fooled by the same girl, after a few days, they both took independence from the same girl. One became "Pandit", and the other became "Jajman".

After a few years, Shri Atal Bihari Vajpayee and Md Firoz Khan reached university, and they both met a girl, the daughter of Shri Pandit Jawaharlal Nehru. One became "Pandit" and the other became "Jajman". Shri Atal Bihari Vajpayee used the term "Durga" for Shrimati Indira inside parliament.

Using even words over any girl comes under teasing, talking even with the girl is witnessed to be the act of teasing, and seeing more than 30 seconds in Delhi comes under teasing.

Every book is a set of past, which becomes variables for the future, wherever we are today, someone else was ever before and someone else will be tomorrow. No one dies ever, no post, no work dies ever.

Ramayana is that "Holy" book, having details of family or is the Pedigree of Ram and Sita. "Sita" herself is the face of Ravan or the daughter of Ravan, Janak, Vibhishan, Kumbh Karan, sister of Akshay Kumar, Meghnath, and others. Or can be said, that "Sita" herself was using "Ravan", and was using others, from her place.

A boy said to a girl, that have no sister and didn't want to fight, so that's why has expected his gift to be returned by courier only, the next moment, the girl's father slapped the boy. Now tell me, who was "Ravan"? And what is "Shiv Tandav Stotram"? Ramayana is that "Holy" book, which has different variables of family. For instance, there was a person, named Shri Moolchand Modi, who had a son named Shri Damodar Das, having a grandson Shri Somabhai Modi. Shri Moolchand Modi was in the place of Raja Aja, Shri Damodar Das was in the place of Dashratha, and Shri Somabhai Modi was in the place of Ram, in that family. After a few years, Shri Damodar Das became the face of Raja Aja, Shri Somabhai Modi became Dashratha, and his son became the face of Ram, in that family, after a few years, Shri Somabhai Modi became the face of Aja, his son became the face of Dashratha, and his grandson became the face of Ram, in that family. Ravan was only an illusion created by "Sita's" family, whereas Janak, himself didn't touch his groom's feet, somewhere, where doing "this and that" with "Sita" somewhere.

Likewise, Shri Dhanka Singh was in the place of Aja, Shri Chhote Singh, was in the place of Dashratha, Shri Rambadan Singh, was in the place of Ram, and after a few years, Shri Chhote Singh became the face of Raja Aja. Shri Rambadan Singh became the face of Raja Dashratha, and his son Shri Yougal Kishore Singh became the face of Ram. After a few years, Shri Rambadan Singh became the face of Aja, Shri Yougal Kishore Singh became the face of Shri Dashratha, and Shri Sachidanand Singh became the face of Ram.

Whosever marriages take place in the court, lawyers are kept for maintaining peace. Permanent lawyers are hired, to maintain the peace. In the marriages that take place at Pandit Ji's doorstep, Pandit Ji takes a salary every month, which means he establishes peace. Marriage is not a disputed thing. He needs to say, about the marriage act. Girls are nothing inside the marriage act. The girl's father and groom have to touch each other's feet. Suppose, She is a widow, having a daughter only. Now, whether her daughter's marriage will happen ever? Or she will become the bride? then whether she and her daughter have to touch his feet too? Which relation will be that? Whether Ravan didn't kidnap that widow? That is why, even fathers-in-law are necessary, and even they have to touch their groom's feet. Inside Ramayana, from Sita's side, Vibhishan touched the feet of their groom and completed the marriage. Not only groom touch the feet of the father-in-law, but, also the father-in-law has to touch the feet of his groom. Girls first have to touch their whole family's feet, then, touch whole In-law's feet, and then in last touches their groom's feet.

➤ Why do "Fathers-in-law" have to touch their feet?

Because they are those, who are living the life after "Jenau", and were using their daughter's face, to provoke "Mahabharata", for robbing their batchmates, somewhere. M.P.'s chair and M.L.A.'s chair are robbed. Interest over interest, the rich become beggars, and the beggar becomes rich. Orphan or Suddar becomes family man, and family man becomes "Suddar". Old becomes young and youth becomes old, Sick becomes fit and fit becomes sick, virtue is stolen. "Bhaduwa" becomes innocent and innocent becomes "Bhaduwa". Girl sitting. Dancing, singing, and posing, on the direction of her suggestion makers. Wherever "Sati" was "Daksha's" daughter yesterday, there "Sati" is someone else today, and someone else will be tomorrow.

➤ What is "Love"?

If "Love" is correct and legal before marriage, then what is the need for marriage or a girl father's to touch their groom's feet? What is the need to go to any temple, mosque, or church? What is the need for "Hawan Kund" for marriage? If "Love" is illegal, then, whether the girl crosses the "Laxman Rekha" or not? Whether boy was accused of teasing the girl or not? Whether the girl, herself provoked for "love" or not? Marriage is that act, girls are nothing inside the marriage act, where the groom touches the feet of the father-in-law, and the father-in-law touches the feet of his groom. The girl is of no use, before touching the girl's father's feet. Marriage is that act. And, coeducation is the place, which is mainly used by Kans, Ravan, to endanger "Krishna", "Ram", somewhere. Ravan, or the girl's father or the girl's family, from one side will start abusing, and slapping, and will do the "Kanya Daan" on the head by mistake or intentionally somewhere, rather than in the feet. Coeducation is that place. And such girls become "Sati" only.

Almost all ladies inside the brothel are victims of "love" before marriage somewhere.

Sati should be auspicious for the place, for the family, not any burden, not any robber, as for what she took birth? Was feeding whom? Was robbing whom? Was disturbing whom? Was spoiling whose image? And why? After all, "Lord Shiva" reached her door, on her words only. Inside the marriage, the girl calls, girl gives the date, not her mother. Wherever "Mother" calls, that means, they were robbing children using their daughter's face only. Whether "Shiv" was knowing, that, for abusing, for disrespecting, for slapping, and for doing "Kanya Daan" on the head, whether "Daksha" has called him?

➤ What is "Love"?

When the first blessing right, remains with the girl's father, inside marriage, there, what is "Love"? The groom touched the feet, and after that, blessing rights changed place, there what is "Love"? Even if, ever, the son of Ram, Love, would have to marry, then also, the marriage act can't be changed. Whatever the illusionary name, but marriage act will not change.

Ramayana is the "Holy book" having the story of "Mahabharata" between, "Ram" and "Sita". Where the girl's father and brother were using "daughter's and sister's" faces and were fighting with "Ram". Was abusing "Maa ki Gaali", where the sieve curses the winnowing basket which in itself has seventy-two holes. What is "Love"? If, Abhimanyu died, inside "Mahabharata". Wherever "Arjun" was earlier, there even "Abhimanyu" was to reach, that means wherever "Ram" was, there even "Love" was to be there. That means, if "Ram" were looking "Malechh, Lafua, Kutta, Maa ki Gaali, Shuddar, Bhaduwa, Rascal, Fail, Fakir", then, even "love" will also look "Malechh, Lafua, Kutta, Maa ki Gaali, Shuddar, Bhaduwa, Rascal, Fail, Fakir" because as the father as the child will be. Whatever the seed, was sown from "Sita's" side, after getting Chocolate, Gift, Ring, that was witnessed by people of society too. That means, by guardians of "Love's" bride too. "Ram" expected, to call, from the "S.T.D" booth, if don't have a mobile or laptop, then did anything wrong? "Mother" will call from the "S.T.D" booth? What is coeducation? Who is dancing there? Girl's mother, became answerer? And this is the fact, that, children are awarded "Fail", that they didn't understand, that, from behind it was cow answering, putting heifer's face ahead.

Suppose a child used the "I love you" phrase over any girl, a girl taking suggestions from her father and mother, that phrase ashamed, made shy to whom? Teased whom? Who replied with their suggestion?

There is a proverb, "As the father, as the son", which means, the son is the face of the father somewhere, in the same way, "As the mother, as the daughter", means, the daughter is the face of the mother somewhere, that is why, inside coeducational institution, they are "Illusion" only.

"Love" means a knife chopped in the back of the family. Knife chopped in the back of elders and juniors. A knife chopped into the groom's back too. Because, she hasn't touched all her guardian's feet, yet, and robbing in the coeducational system. She is that thing. If she has "Love", then what is her future? Future, full of violence, only. "Pandit" and "Jajman" are those things. Whatever "Jajman" was expecting, was given to "Pandit". "Surpankha's" whole life, lapsed in taking revenge with her brother. Wherever the girl and boy admitted that they "Loved each other". Marry them, following all marriage acts. Otherwise, she will become wretched for the family, wherever she will be, wherever she will live. Can't kill, because no one dies, the soul remains alive.

Coeducation is the place, where girl while dancing, gives the signal to "Pandit" and even gives the signal to "Jajman" too. The girl, on the one hand, is called "Pandit", and on the other hand called "Jajman". Like Draupadi, asking about, whom to select and whom to reject from Krishna. That means, it was "Krishna" who was selecting and rejecting, using the face of "Draupadi". Rejected "Karan", and "Duryodhan" and accepted "Arjun", "Karan" died, and "Abhimanyu" died. Suppose "Karan" and "Duryodhan" are alive, and "Abhimanyu" is also alive, then whether "Abhimanyu" will touch "Karan's" and "Duryodhan's" feet or not for their blessings. "Arjun" even married "Krishna's" sister too. That means, "Arjun" married that person's sister too, who was suggesting "Draupadi" inside "Mahabharata". Was suggesting "Draupadi" and married her sister with "Arjun" in "Mahabharata". "Krishna's" own sister became co-wife of "Arjun".

Coeducation is that place, where, a girl's brothers are benefited. Because, there all batchmate's life is stolen somewhere, and are served to their brother, while giving them "Swear, Pledge", that "India is my country, and all Indians are my brothers and sisters…" Girl, doing grooming of whom, while dancing and posing? Who becomes "King" there? "Dhrishtadyumna" used "Draupadi" for spoiling her own life in all aspects. What is "Draupadi"? Any reward? Which reward? Became the reason for "Mahabharata", then became the reason for partition, and in last her son died. Whether she was any reward? Which award? "Kans" ruler of 7 gotras, became "King", and "Vasudev", ruler of 11 gotras, was in prison. Shakuni married her sister to somewhere else, even after "Love" before marriage. "Ravan" killed his sister's husband.

There was a "King" having a son and a daughter, whose daughter was in "Love" with someone, inside the coeducational system, after a few days, he and his son and others in their family killed their daughter's friend and married her daughter with someone else, then shed crocodile tears in front of his daughter telling that, his kidney has failed. After that, the daughter's kidney was removed. First killed her friend, first killed someone's son, someone's brother's then married her somewhere else, then removed her kidney. Later her daughter gave birth to a daughter. And if as the father, as the child, if as the mother, as the daughter, then whether his daughter was her mother's face? Whether her daughter will be her face or not?

This is the condition of "Love" before marriage, because "Sensor" lies everywhere.

Coeducation is the place where batchmates are kept in the place of brothers while giving them "swear", that they "all are brother and sisters" And the biggest drama happens between "brother and sister" only. "Sisters are used for robbing batchmates by guardians, and later those special guardians give everything to their brother".

Tutankhamun married his cousin's sister. In Islam, even, brothers and sisters are married, who haven't drunk milk from the same breast. Brother of girl are those things. Krishna was proclaimed brother of Draupadi, but, he married his sister with Arjun. He was the maternal uncle of "Abhimanyu", and "Abhimanyu" died. He was in the place of "Kans" for "Abhimanyu", somewhere.

But, In Hindu, In Brahman Bhumihaar, the past six gotras are relatives, and the remaining six gotras are for marriage, among whom has to select one, considering the total gotra to be 13.

Madam Jayalalitha, Mamta, Indira, Sonia, Menika, and Surpankha are those, who considered "Love" to be "Legal", whereas, disobeyed the marriage act somewhere, where, "Love" can happen, after marriage only. That means after the groom's feet are touched, in "Hindi" it is called "Pair Pujai". After "Pair Pujai" "Love" happens. First, they touched all body parts of the groom, then touched the elder brother and sister's feet. And their father didn't touch their groom's feet. What is "Love"?

Wherever the girl does "love" before marriage, that becomes wretched for that home, wherever she gets married, because she will never or can't reply to the phrase "I love you", because her tongue is chopped, because she already had given words to someone else. They will act mentally all the time. Whoever they given the chance of "I love you" takes benefit of that, Whether "Love" happens first, and the guardian will bless later, or the guardian will bless first, then "Love" will happen? First "Pair Pujai" will happen, or first "Love" will happen?

> What is "Love Marriage"?

Both the parties admitted, that went out of home, and went to school, college, university, and offices for teasing, trapping boys, robbing, and vice-versa. Were FIRs of teasing not filed inside the police station, inside the court, or in front of the school's management, and that turned in "Love Marriage" or not? They became over-talented. Where someone kept silent, over someone's act, and that turned into marriage, according to their need only. Where "FIR' was not filed. "FIR" means "First attempt at Raping", somewhere. What do local police do, that is not hidden? In the fight between girl and boy, either head breaks or bed breaks. Debating is also a way of fighting. Complaining is also a way of fighting. That is why, coeducation should be checked seriously, somewhere. That grooming of whom happens?

Wherever "Love" gets passed easily, by guardians, their other junior starts copying them from one hand and teasing batchmates from the other hand. the younger sister didn't touch the elder sister's or elder brother's feet, there, what did she do? Who is she, inside the marriage? Nothing. She is the only spoiler of batch, and society, wherever she goes, only will abuse, curse, and do nothing, only will be found posing, and disobeying, and will be found only robbing sight, property, and respect. With their act. If you want to marry your daughter by deception, or fraud, if want to become any "Daksha, or Ravan" then start reciting a wonderful mantra, start chanting on a biscuit worth rupees five or a plastic ring worth eight annas, like "Malechh, Lafua, Kutta, Maa Ki Gaali, Mental, Shuddar, Bhaduwa, Rascal, Fail, Beggar" and slap, Like any vegetable seller while selling vegetables says like a mantra, "Take potatoes, take lady's finger, take bitter gourd, take a pumpkin, take coriander and take chili". Just like that, start chanting wonderful mantras of abuse "Malechh, Lafua, Kutta, Maa Ki Gaali, Mental, Shuddar, Bhaduwa, Beggar, Rascal, Fail", what is the maximum he will do? Will he expect his feet to be touched by all? Even then the marriage will take place. Especially, when the elder daughter had "Love" before marriage in other castes. Slap him, using his energy, and become "Baali", using own daughter's face, using dancing puppets and different dancing postures. Wherever the elder daughter made a mistake, and then start abusing juniors, and their batchmates, for paying down their voice. Then start spoiling and robbing "Juniors". And start spoiling their mood of having "Love" in their life. Who doesn't know, that, no father can bear the rejection of their daughter at the stage of marriage, that is why they use the coeducational system, to spoil their future, and present, that is why those special illusionary numbers are awarded inside the educational system. A child given chocolate in class 8th, 9th, 11th, 12th, having no source of income, celebrated birthday only, whether did anything wrong? The girl's father's, and others started chanting "Malechh, lafua, Mental, Kutta, Maa ki gaali, Shuddar, Bhaduwa, Rascal, Fail, Beggar". Like he was any criminal? He was slapped and beaten, why? If beating anyone, slapping anyone, disrespecting anyone, then, please note, as the father will be as the son will be, that means, somewhere sown the seed of beating daughter's son too, slapping daughter's son too, disrespecting daughter's son too. Maybe that is why Lord Shiva married Devi Parvati.

The daughter will touch her father's feet first, or the groom's feet first? Younger sister will touch, her elder brother's feet first, or groom's feet first?

The full moon happens every 28th day, which means, on the same day, "Purnima" happens, which means, Brahman comes, which means, somewhere, same day, he takes salary every month. For becoming "Pandit" and for making "Jajman". Because, the girl copied her elder sister from one hand and teased her batchmate too, and that became "Pandit" and Jajman's" theory. Pandit is "Love" of "Devi" and "Jajman" is the writer. The term Political Pandit is used, whether they feel proud or not. Whether his wife, will ask him, to, pay them, and pay them? Who is she? Her brother didn't give her rights, scolded her from her property earned by robbing schoolmates, batchmates, somewhere, and expected what from, the home, where she became a homemaker? Expect what from batchmate, schoolmate, collegemate? Husband are any note-printing machines? Throw some notes here and throw some notes there, throw some notes in "Falana's" function, throw some notes in transportation for attending those functions. Shri Manmohan Singh, Former prime minister of India, already had said, that money doesn't grow on trees. It is said, that, on full moon night, all "God" becomes alive. Who takes a salary every full moon? Who is God? Child or Pandit ji? "Jajman" or "Pandit"? If any child can be abused, then what should be done with Pandit Ji? If any child can be praised with words like "Malechh, Lafua, Kutta, Maa ki Gaali, Mental, Shuddar, Bhaduwa, Fail, Beggar", then how people and others should praise "Pandit Ji"? Because, they are those, by nature, about whom, even writers know while writing, that, they will be reading. That means, the writer was knowing, that, which worship they do. They are even called "Political Pandits". But, such chanting, worshipping book, Holy Book, is expected from the writer, because, the "Political Pandit" doesn't even know how to worship.

Through the mouth of the reader, who becomes alive, through those assembled words through any Holy Books?

➤ Why such "Holy Books" are expected to be wrote?

Because of "Holika's" act somewhere. And other reason may would be, that whatever writer wrote, the same even reader would read. Whatever "Jajman" wrote, "Brahman" will read the same. If writer was abused, then Brahman should be also abuse. "Pandit" and "Jajman" is like "Co-husband", because of a dancing puppet. If dancing puppets can decide, "Pandit and Jajman" theory, then whether writer can decide "Sati and Parvati" system or not?

In some areas, the "Father-in-law", and "Son-in-law" play Kabaddi, and Kusti, and touch each other's feet, and the marriage completes. But, the child doesn't want to fight with Evil Ravan, Evil Daksha, Replying to them over their words like "Malechh, Lafua, Kutta, Mental, Maa ki Gaali, Shuddar, Bhaduwa, Rascal, Fail, Beggar" is like throwing a stone in the mud.. They are those things. What to marry, in those families, who are accused of Rape, murder, robbery, extortion, smuggling, prostitution, disturbing marriages, robbing brides". They are not for any marriage. This is a punishment, for their past in the present, so that, they can correct their future. Ravan, great-grandson of Bramha. Whether Bramha feels proud or not, when he witnesses that their great grandson, is accused of "Rape, Murder, Robbery, extortion, smuggling, disturbing marriages, robbing brides"? Whether he feel proud? Whether he feels proud or not, while describing them, among other gods, like Vishnu, Lord Shiva, among Surya Dev, who are involved in "Rape, murder, robbery, extortion, smuggling, disturbing marriages, robbing brides"? Whether he feel proud? Whether "Sarswati" feels proud, when anyone does love marriage?

Whether "Sarswati" feels proud, when anyone uses the phrase "I love you" before marriage, over a dozen of girls? Whether "Saraswati" feels, that, after having "Love" before marriage, the girl's father will touch his groom's feet? Whether she take any guarantee? Which business do they run, while stealing life from anyone's door? Whether they feel proud or not? Ram will have "Jenau"? That means, whether "Ram" will become "Bhaduwa"? Asks to time, that, whether "Ram" will become "Bhaduwa"? The moment, "Ram" is made "Bhaduwa" what do they make to "Sita"? Intentionally. Asks to Time. For saving whom? Bhagat Singh died around the age of 25. More than 50 countries read, the behavior done by the door of dancing puppets.

This child is Ram.

Whether this child needs "Jenau"? If the child in the second photo will be given "Jenau", then whether "Spear" of "Surya Dev" will hurt "Vasudev's" head too or not? Jesus was hanged on the Cross. In Islam, people beat themselves with "Hunter" during Moharram.

This is the truth of "Jenau". That means, someone intentionally tried to kill the child using school, to kill the Vasudev using school or not? Whether this child know any words? Who feeds them "I love you" phrase? Who sent them, teaching the phrase inside the coeducational system? Who was playing from behind?

The child in your home is "Ram".

The day, these children will have their "Sita, Laxmi, Parvati, Saraswati" in their curdle, that day, will be the day of happiness, and prosperous life will begin.

Everyone wants to know, that, what "Ram' has given to "Sita" in his writing expectation. He somewhere, expected his gift to be couriered. Hanuman was used for returning his ring, and expected her to marry with them, whomever she provoked for "Love".

➤ What is fighting?

Once Vaayu Putra Hanuman and Lord Parshuram fought, "Hanuman" was losing, the moment, Hanuman touched the feet of Lord Parshuram, he won. The fight is only about touching feet or pulling anyone into feet.

Bramha sent a chariot, and after seeing that special chariot all women came out. Full marriage story. Wherever such extraordinary acts happen, of making "Bhaduwa", there girl, remains barren for her whole life. Because she is only a "Sati", planted on the head. Wherever "Sati" was someone else yesterday, today someone else is, and tomorrow someone else will be, because, donkeys are also reading and acting, posing of reading. Wherever writer was yesterday, someone else is today, and someone else will be tomorrow.

How is it possible, that the same set of Gaali is used over different-different children from the "girl or Ravan" side? How? Whether Bramha's hand is involved or not? Saraswati's tongue is involved or not? How word arrows are used, whether he knows or not? He "Failed", in becoming "Bhaduwa"? Word arrows are used from the girl's family's side or not, suggestions are given. Who was responsible for Mr. Bamula's death, in the country, where below 25% of people can write any application? 75% of people's homes remain safe, their children are safe, and Mr. Bamula died. Whether children make mistakes that enter any educational system?

Wherever the wife ditches, the husband never earns. He leaves earning. Why to earn? Why? For whose son? Why feed children, when Bali, uses their power, to beat children? For selling what? For making what? "Prostitute" and "Bhaduwa"? The boy pulls all the power of "Bali, Ravan, Daksha" chops their tongue, and hand, and pulls their navel for every birth. The child has taken birth, and every month, god, and evil become alive. Why read such "Holy Books", where god and evil both come alive? "Jajman" is god or "Pandit" is god for "Devi"? One is god, and one is Evil. Every 28ᵗʰ day, who becomes alive? Why use anyone's mouth, for reading those books? Whether "Love Babu", or "Reader Babu", went to school, to make "Prostitute and Bhaduwa"? Father and mother sent them, for this to any school? Whether, evil groups, great grandchildren of Bramha, go to school to make "Bhaduwa and Prostitute"? Who is Ravan? It is said, "As the father, as the child, that means, as the grandfather, as the grandchild, that means, as the great grandfather, as the great-grandchildren, then If Ravan was "Evil", then what Bramha is? Whether Bramha feels proud or not? Does Ravan have any capability of feeding his own family? What does he do? Does Ravan have the capability of even "Kaudi"? Dogs are better than Ravan. In the words of Salman Khan, Dogs are better than girls. Whoever founds giving any blessing to "Ravan", except death, chop their hand, chop their legs, chop their hands, pull their navel. What is Ravan? Storyteller hired for the entertainment of "Lord Ganesha"? The staff of Lord Shiva? The employee of Lord Shiva? Why did Ravan search groom for "Surpankha" after killing her husband? Spoiled her past in the present, and spoiled future somewhere. Expert in spoiling the past, in the present, and designing the future. When "Love" is correct, then why kill "Surpankha's" husband? The evil group's leader, himself should answer in his own words. Bramha should answer in their own words. Whether girl's "Jenau" happens? Boy "Jenau" and girl's "Surgery" are the same thing somewhere. But, wherever, guardians are killed, and prostitutes are used, for making "Bhaduwa", there what children should do? One side robbed "Ram" and the other side robbed Sita/Sati too. Tricked in 4% rate of interest, for what? For robbing wife? The child is happy to live unmarried. Because, from Evil's door, from Sita's door, was tricked. That means she was allowing her family members and others to rob her. She was that shameless. What a coincidence, that both Ram and Laxman married with two sisters!!! Nicely used coeducational school or not? School is any marriage bureau? Where information is leaked by management. A child's home's landline number was leaked by the school's management. For what? Whether he didn't pay fees? The girl leaked his number to someone to abuse. Ram left Sita's illusion of attraction, where he "Failed" and she topped, and married Parvati. Suppose "Parvati" is fully illiterate, then also, "topper girl having a shinning degree" has no rights over her husband. Like after getting chocolate or a gift, using the daughter's face, the girl's mother starts becoming the bride, starts suggesting, the girl's father starts suggesting, and robbing, time, money, and respect using that towel.

There is a song from "Salman Khan's" movie, "Hum Aapke Hain Kaun" where, there is a line from Salman Khan, "If you are doesn't become mine, then, I will become priest or saint", where "Madhuri Dixit" replies or allows him to become priest or saint and says him to "Come home for having Dakshina".

What is trust in the girl? The girl is just a face of illusion inside the marriage act. Talking to her is just a waste of time. Waste of respect, and a waste of property, because, inside the marriage act, blessing rights change place. The home where they take birth, that home is not her home, which means, they take birth "Beghar" and expect other's to beg. Girls are like those "Amjad Khan" of Mr. Natwar Lal, where he sings the song "No one's stomach is filled with loud talks, whoever salutes us, never dies hungry, crazy will die, fighting with us is foolishness", as they pay for reading or for teasing "Kaikei was very beautiful" and "Something like Sita". but the fact is whoever has trust in Ram never dies Hungry. For example, women themselves pay, to tease them, for reading "Sundar Kand", and that "Kaikei" was very beautiful. Does that mean women are like "Amjad Khan" of the movie Mr. Natwar Lal, or not? Especially In the movie, "Amjad Khan" was in-law's family of Amitabh Bachchan.

In Sholay, Amjad Khan was in the in-law's family of Dharmendra. Or can be said in the place of Ravan somewhere.

There is another movie by Amitabh Bachchan, "Saudagar", where, whenever his wife did make-up, he faced losses. That means, on every 28ᵗʰ day, when "Political Pandit" comes, and 'devi' does make-up, "Jajman" faces lose, somewhere.

There is another movie by Amitabh Bachchan, "Suryavansham", where, he abuses, and disrespects his child, saying to his wife, that, "Look, we haven't given him any toy for playing in his childhood days, now he is playing with our sentiments".

Trusting a girl means spoiling the future in the present. They are those, things. When any girl or her family spoils her daughter's life and disrespects her groom, that means, sown the seed of disrespecting their groom's children too. For example, "Abhimanyu" died. Either don't run a coeducational system, or don't disrespect anyone's child, or don't give them any swear like "India is my country, and all Indians are my brothers and sisters". Other's children are "Malechh, Lafua, Mental, Kutta, Maa ki Gaali, Shuddar, Fail, Bhaduwa, Beggar"? What own children are? What, they are? Girl's respect is respect, and boys are "Malechh, Lafua, Kutta, Mental, Maa ki Gaali, Shuddar, Fail, Bhaduwa, Beggar"? Girls are those things, whoever will fight for, them, will rob them and will disrespect them only. Whoever chooses them, they disrespects them and abuse them, only. While abusing these words, any girl's family disrespects anyone's pedigree. Pedigree, means, whole upcoming and past, whole future and past. For a successful life, please stay away from the girl, and their family. As, much, distance, that much success.

> ➤ Dog mating happens for over rupees ten thousand for some breeds, then, what is "love"?

Coeducation is a place, where married children are also coming, not using "Vermilion", and are fooling other children. Teachers are also students, where they read, and do discussions over any topic. Some teachers had also witnessed teasing students, and later they married their students.

> ➤ What is the marriage system?

"Bharat" touched "Ram's" feet, "Laxman" touched "Ram's" feet, Shatrughan touched Ram's feet, now, "Love and Kush" have to touch "Bharat's", "Laxman's", "Shatrughan's" feet for their blessings. That means, considering "Love and Kush" to be "Ram's" face, later the "disguised face of Ram" even have to touch their father's brother's feet. This is the system. That means, "Pandu" touched "Dhritrashtra's feet", now, "Dhritrashtra's children" were to touch "Pandu's feet", and "Pandu's" children were to touch "Dhritrashtra's" children's feet, according to their age. And, unmarried children's feet are not touched, because they take blessings, not give blessings.

The child pulls all lives stolen from "Chidaai Pariwaar", Brahman Bharadwaj Bhumihaar's family while using "Dancing puppets", inside the coeducational system. Pulls all rights of living on earth.

Virtue is stolen, place of brother-in-law and groom are interchanged, when anyone abuses "Malechh, Lafua, Kutta, Mental, Maa ki Gaali, Shuddar, Bhaduwa, Rascal, Fail", when anyone is expected to have swear or pledge that "India is my country, and all Indians are my brothers and sisters..". "Ram" are made "Bhaduwa", and "Bhaduwa" are made Ram. Because Shani Dev is considered to be a decorator of life. Marksheet, are decorated, and long life are given by Shani Dev, too. Ravan was that character, who kept Shani Dev under his foot, which made a negative impact on their children too. From whomever, long life was to be earned, they kept them under their feet. To get any blessing, people have to bow down or have to touch their feet. Suppose the child is "Shani Dev", and can decorate anyone's mark sheet or can decorate an experience certificate on paper, for playing with the eyeballs of readers, for using someone's mouth for playing with ears, but, forgetting "Long Life" they have to touch, his feet. Ravan's act of keeping Shani Dev under his foot made that much negative impact on their children, that, even their children, Meghnath, Akshay Kumar, and others tried the same. And, that is why, they never got a "Long Life". And inside coeducation, "Meghnath, Akshay Kumar, Kans, Shakuni" all rob Ram, in all aspects. The groom's and brother-in-law's places are interchanged. That is why, maybe "Sita/Sati" even didn't get any long life from "Ram". Because of the seed sown from her, after getting gifted, complaining, gossiping, and spying, all are acts of killing someone.

There is a story, Once "truth", and "Lie" were going somewhere. "Lie," said, let's have a bath, the moment they went into the lake, lie ran away, taking Truth's all dresses. From that day, "lie" has been roaming in the world, wearing true "clothes". That means, for saving someone, and for interchanging the place, a child's place was interchanged. The virtue of truth was stolen, somewhere by the lie. In saving "Bhaduwa", someone was made "Bhaduwa", using a girl. Simple question, if anyone were ever to become any "Bhaduwa", then, whether he randomly, use the "I Love You" phrase over some girls or not? What is "Jenau"? and what is "Chumaan"? Evil and God, both were called by "Devi", and time fulfilled her demand. "Evil" became "Political Pandit", and god became "Jajman". Both were expected from the "Navel" of "Devi" only, while her dancing activity. Ravan's navel was having "Nectar" for him, but what about a girl's Navel? Girls are also the face of Ravan. "Sita" was sister of "Surpankha".

Inside "Mahabharata" Krishna was fighting, and Krishna was dying too. Inside "Ramayana", "Ram" was fighting and Ram was dying. Whole life was coming from Ram, and was going to Ram. They were creator and destroyers too.

Girls are not supposed to see above knees, there who tried to bless any child using the terms "Malechh, Lafua, Kutta, Maa Ki Gaali, Shuddar, Bhaduwa, Rascal, Fail, Beggar"? Surpankha's family members? Expert in ruining the smartness of males. Nature of "Surpankha" and Ravan be the same or not? Expert in ruining the smartness of males by their "Ascetic act" somewhere.

"Sataisa" child, didn't cross "Sataisa", there, who tried to kill that child at the age of 12,14,16,20,25? Who? Why? Life is of 100 birthdays, from the eyes of god, every year is of one day only. So had expected 100 years of a healthy, wealthy, prosperous life for the family, considering the year to be 365 days, that means, 36525 days, considering days to be of year for the Brahman Bharadwaj Bhumihaar's family.

Girls are faces of "Laxmi, Saraswati, Puja, Kali, Chandika, Durga, Parvati, Sanjana, Riddhi, Siddhi, Neelima, Rukmani", but, they should not accuse any batchmates, they should accuse their father and brother only. Batchmates are not responsible for their marriage. Her father and brother should think. Batchmate's home's life, money, and respect are robbed while sitting with them. The girl is only a gossiping device only, inside the educational system. Boy done this, boy done that. "Falana" boy has a four-wheeler, "Falana" boy has this property, They are those things. burner of own, and others home too, while gossiping, complaining, spying. They are those talented things.

What is friendship with girls inside the coeducational system? What is friendship with boys inside the coeducational system? It is a waste of time, money, respect, and life. Batchmate will retire almost around the same time only. But Bhagat Singh died around the age of 25. Wherever, any girl, disrespects any boy, wherever any girl's family disrespects any boy, that means, they disrespected that child's whole pedigree, somewhere. Evil Daksha, disrespected Lord Shiva, then whether disrespected Lord Ganesha or not? When "Karan" was disrespected by Draupadi and her suggestion makers, then whether disrespected the whole family of "Karan" or not? Whether sown the seed of disrespect for the niece of "Karan's" or not? Whether, "Abhimanyu" was to touch "Karan's" feet or not, if they both were alive, then "Draupadi" herself sowed, the seed of disrespect for her children in the future or not when she disrespected "Karan" on the direction of suggestion makers? The elder brothers of "Yuddhisthir, Arjun, Bhim, Nakul, Sahdev" were "Shuddar or Sud Putra", where "Sieve curses the winnowing basket, who in itself has seventy-two holes, thief scolding the police", then who was "Sud Putra or Shuddar"? What is "Shuddar"? Before "Jenau" all are "Shuddar" and after "Jenau" all are "Bhaduwa". Where, girls are not supposed to speak, then wherever, they speak, are breaking the "Law", somewhere, either by crossing the "Laxman Rekha", or by teasing, and provoking. The girl herself should answer, , what they are, where even their father has to touch their groom's feet, to complete the marriage, there, what they are? It is a boy's discipline, who doesn't use the "I love you" phrase over them, before marriage. The home, in which they take birth, that home is not their home, what they are? They are only life-stealing machines. By birth, they are "Beghar". What is "Love"? Wherever "Love" held, their brother had killed their lovers. As, till when having "Laxmi" in the pocket, till having "Saraswati", till having "Puja", "Laxmi" over, "Sarswati" over, and "Puja" complete, that means, till when having "Money" in the pocket, till then have the drama of "Love, friendship", till having drama of having "hi, hi, hi, hi" in any photo, till then have "enjoyment, party", "Money" over, "Love, friendship" over, "Enjoyment, Party" over, "hi, hi, hi, hi" over. It is like "Give money, and listen story". Expenditure is yours and the story of someone else.

When "Poverty" comes from the door, "Love" jumps from the "window" and runs away.

There is my setting with god, neither he calls me, nor do I go to meet him, God lies in all five elements, god lies in surroundings, and no one dies ever. "Lord Vishnu" is still on the globe, "Lord Shiva" is still on the globe, wherever, we are today, someone else was ever before, and someone else will be tomorrow. That means, ten centuries ago, "Vishnu" were "Vasudev", and five centuries ago, "Vasudev" were "Narayan", and two centuries ago "Narayan" was "Ram". That means, ten centuries ago, "Lord Shiva" was "Neelkanth", five centuries ago, "Neelkanth" was "Shankar", two centuries ago, "Shankar" was "Bhole".

There is my setting with god, neither he calls me, nor I go to meet. The patient has their setting with god, but neither he calls them, nor they go to meet, the Doctor has their setting with god, neither, they call them, nor they go to meet, children have their setting with god, neither they call them, nor they go to meet, teacher have their setting with god, neither they call them, nor they go to meet, Customer have their setting with god, neither they call them, nor they go to meet, seller have their setting with god, neither they call them, nor they go to meet, Sleeping person have their setting with god, neither they call them, nor they goes to meet, guard have their setting with god, neither they call them, nor they go to meet. Brahman have their setting with god, neither, they call them, nor they go to meet, Dom have their setting with god, neither, they calls them, nor they goes to meet. Dead bodies have their setting with god, neither they call them, nor do they go to meet. Animals have their setting with god, neither they call them, nor do they go to meet. Ashes have their setting with god, neither they call them, nor do they go to meet. God has their setting with devotees, neither they call them, nor they go to meet. God lies in all five elements. God lies in the chair, on which we sit. Till then have "Laxmi", till then the system is working, "Laxmi" over, all setting over.

No one dies ever. Shri Mohandas Karamchand Gandhi is still on the globe, Pandit Jawaharlal Nehru is still on the globe, Shri Bala Saheb Thackeray is still on the globe, Shri Rajeev Gandhi is still on the globe, Shri Sanjay Gandhi is still on the globe. Vishnu Dev is still on the globe, Mahadev is still on the globe, Wherever I am today, someone else was ever before, and someone else will be tomorrow. No words, No posts, no work dies ever, wherever we are today, someone else was ever before and someone else will be tomorrow. That means, the act of having a personal setting with all gods means, all evils means, all future dead souls, all past dead souls means, wherever I am today, someone else was ever before, and someone else will be tomorrow.

Do the work, don't think about the fruit, work is worship, and work is god's offerings.

For me, every temple is just a monument, a grave. "Taj Mahal" is the grave of Mumtaz. Abusing even a "Grave" and abusing a "temple", or "Mosque", or "Church", abusing dead bodies in mortuaries, abusing Ashes, abusing history books, abusing Holy books, abusing even orphans, abusing even them, in whosever home someone had died, will result in the same. If somewhere, his great grandfather died, then somewhere in someone's home, he has taken birth, by nature. Population always remains the same on the globe.

> ➤ Why girl's father even have to touch the groom's feet?

Pandit Jawaharlal Nehru's daughter, met two males during her education, one Shri Atal Bihari Vajpayee, and the other Md Firoz Khan. and married Md Firoz Khan. But, Pandit Jawaharlal Nehru didn't touch the feet of his groom. Md Firoz Khan, died on September 8, 1960, whereas, Pandit Jawaharlal Nehru died on 27 may 1964. Almost four years later, his Father-in-law died. Another example is "Shri Rajeev Gandhi died on 21 May 1991 and father-in-law died almost around there only. Whatever the reasons, someone, intentionally ate those acts, and where girl's father even had to touch the groom's feet. In some marriages, the groom died around 40-50, and the father-in-law crossed 70 easily. Wife crossed 80 easily. Husband died. Because someone ate their marriage act. Or can be said, someone changed the groom's place, intentionally, with "Father-in-law" or "brother-in-law" somewhere. Where it is taught, inside the school, that "All countrymen are my brothers and sisters", how "Love" could happen? Batchmates are "Sati". Batchmates are Shiv, who earn "FAIL" from their batchmates inside the coeducation system, by their dear ones or face of "Sarswati". They realize, that they can spoil their mark sheets and certificates, and opportunities of having any job, through their extra-curricular activities, like "Singing", "Dancing", and "complaining" and can even use their father for disrespect. They are those things. It is very necessary to even teach, through schooling, especially in the coeducation system, that "Sita" died around the age of 42-45, below 50, below menopause situation. Otherwise, some women's husbands died twenty years ago, and they faced cervical cancer after two decades.

Wherever a girl's father denies touching his groom's feet, please marry your children with someone else. She will become "Sati" only. "Sati" means "Mata Sati". Inside marriage girls are considered to be in the place of the "moon" The first moon of any child is his mother, and then that place his wife takes. That means the moon changes place, somewhere. the child remains fixed at his birthplace.

The donation which happens in the temple, on that government have their rights. The whole country fought for Independence, then whether they paid taxes or not? In making temples, whole countries pay taxes. Schools, Colleges, University, all are paying "Taxes", all are the place of god, then also they are also paying "Taxes". No one donates schools, colleges, universities, or temples, after constructing them. Whether they even should pay taxes or not, where all are beggars? Where all are begging? This revenue collected from the donation from the country, or from abroad, will be used, for the development purposes of the poor then, the country will also feel burden-free. Those amounts can be used for constructing charitable hospitals, schools, colleges, and universities. Daily in India, Over thousands of crores are donated inside different temples collectively.

If the donation of the temple, will be used for the benefit of the country, then, even in the tea-seller's home, children will have "Maggie", on different occasions, easily. "Achchhe Din or Good Day" will come for the country.

To reduce the tax burden, on countries, to increase GDP, the Government should even take control over the daily incomes in temples. Brahman and others should be hired on "Salary". Like Dom is hired to maintain the register on different Ghats. They are getting a "Salary" for the work, they do. Brahman should also pay taxes, on their own. Tax gives them the benefits, of having loans for flats or vehicles, or for other purposes, from government bodies. "If the child is good, then why to accumulate wealth, if the child is bad, then why to accumulate wealth"?

Tax is a government right. That means, whether marriage happens in court or not? Why only a temple? Just because, of the act, where even a girl father has to touch the feet of his groom.

Tax is like "Dakshina", and is like salary. Where, those taxes are used, for their safety, for their development, and their services. Tax is that thing. The government has the right to take "Taxes" but, for what? On behalf of Taxes, what do they serve? Daily, thousands of news are coming through the newspaper. Disrespecting anyone doesn't make them over-smart. People who are themselves the most disrespected personalities, from where they will learn to respect anyone? From where?

Have you ever noticed that two animals are left to fight, and are made wild, not fit for living in a home? Can't be petted by humans, as humans are also animals. Cow, Horse, Dog, Elephant, Ox, Bull, Lion, tiger, Cat, leopard, Eagle, Vulture, Hawk, Falcon, Fox, Crow, fish, hippopotamus, Crocodile, Giraffe, etc all can pet them, but no human can be petted. One is evil, and the other is god, one is "Pandit" and the other is "Jajman", evil and god are made to fight. There intentionally, some targeted children are made wild, by abusing and slapping, "Malechh, Lafua, Kutta, Maa ki gaali, Shuddar, Bhaduwa, Rascal, Fail", for making them wild somewhere. those children were not looking good, they were made wild. Yes of course god will win. Evil can't win. Wherever "Evil" won, there corruption, extortion, murder, and all such businesses grow. Wherever god, won, peace happens. There is a village "Shani Shignapur" in Maharashtra, where, people don't lock their gates, place of "Shani Dev", It is said that Shani Dev himself takes care of their Home, Shops, Property, and them too.

Dead people's products are not used, the soul has their sentiments with those products. Like women's ornaments, and men's land, vehicles, or property. Until and unless they haven't assigned them. If will disturb anyone, then will earn disturbance.

For People of the 25th century, today is what? For people of the 25th century, "Prabhu Shri Ram's" temple is what? Which act is that? Act from the Past, or Act from the 26th century? Act in the

25th century, on the name of Ram, will be what? "Act" from the past", "Act" from the 21st century, or Act from the 26th century? "Act" from "Future" or "Act" from "Past"? like in the 90s, the construction was acted in "Future", or "act" from "Past". People of the 22nd, 23rd, 25th, and 50th centuries, will say what about the construction? Shri Mohandas Karamchand Gandhi came first or did Prabhu Shri Ram temple come? Shirdi Sai, came first, or Prabhu Shri Ram's temple was constructed earlier, Ramayana was written earlier, or temple was constructed earlier?

Just as a Guru gives education to everyone, passes the exam, but does not give education to his child, he always hires another teacher for him, in the same way, no Brahmin can get his son married, for that He will always keep other Brahmins. Because Ramayana itself is the book of mantra for marriage.

Leaves to them to answer, who said, that "Prabhu Shri Ram" took birth at the place, wherever the temple was constructed, and whether people will stop celebrating "Ramnaumi"? Brahmans will stop going home during "Ramnaumi"? Brahman will stop doing door to door campaign on "Ramnaumi"? Whether, on Ramnaumi, there will be no birth in any hospital or any poor's home? Whether, those saint's, priest's grandchildren are faces of Ram in their family or not? Whether they are in the place of Aja or not in their life? Whoever is in any temple? No politics should be done, in the name of Ram, because "Ram" is in himself the "King" and in the name of "King" politics doesn't suit, if anywhere, anyone does politics in the name of "Ram", then, that means, they chops knife in "King's" back. Politics suits to "King" only, on their name, politics are not done. Shri Somabhai Modi was in the place of Ram and shri Damodar Das Modi was in the place of Dashratha, and Shri Moolchand Modi was in the place of Aja. Ram changes place too. Shri Damodar Das was in the place of Aja, Shri Somabhai Modi was in the place of Dashratha, then Shri Amrit Modi became the face of Ram. As said, Ram changes the place too, Shri "Somabhai Modi" was in the place of Aja, then Shri Amrit Modi became "Dashratha", and then Shri Narendra Modi became Ram in that family. Ram changes place too, like "Shani Dev" changes place too.

Now, as the temple has been constructed on charity, and is open for public visit and for charity and donation, He appreciates too, that, wow, what a temple has been constructed in the country. Hopes, that regular checking from different agencies will occur, of those ornaments, and statues. As, when people are experts in robbing virtue, then, what to say, about those ornaments, statues? In the movie "Gopi Kishan", "Suresh Oberoi" was made accused of stealing ornaments and statues from the temple. Wow, hoping, that from today, the tax burden from the country will be reduced. Hoping, that from today, Prabhu Shri Ram's temple will even share some burden of civilians, hoping that, from the donations, some charitable hospitals will be inaugurated, hoping from the donations, some schools, colleges, and universities, will be established. Hoping, that from the donations, some people will have at least two times meals. From the charity collected every year, that will be a great help to the country, as the country has contributed to the construction, which will have increasing religious values with time.

Only they will use Hunters, Stick, Bullets, Arms, or will shout or trick, who themselves don't have any logic, in their discussion or their debate. Will do "Fail" on the answer, where it is written, to answer in own words only. If has to answer in their own words, then how he failed? He answered in his own words. "Fail" means, what?

Whoever tries to disturb or disobey, or to disrespect any family members of "Chidaai Pariwaar", please make them "Landless, Powerless, speechless, tongueless, hand less, toothless, word less, Navel less". Whoever founds disrespecting "Bharat", please make them, "Landless, Powerless, Speechless, tongue less, hand less, teethless, wordless, Navel Less". Whoever tries to disrespect Ram, please make them "Landless, Powerless, Speechless, tongue less, Hand less, teethless, wordless, Navel Less". whoever tries to steal those ornaments, those statues, Prays to Vulture, Prays to Snake, prays to scorpion, prays to leeches, prays to frogs, prays to tiger, prays to foxes, prays to deer, prays to peacock, prays to ants, prays to mouse, prays to elephant, prays to cows, prays to buffalos, prays to dogs, prays to cats, prays to lizards, prays to horses, prays to camels, prays to giraffe, prays to leopards, prays to bears, prays to kangaroos, prays to monkeys, prays to mongooses, prays to pig, prays to eagle, prays to falcon, prays to swan, prays to crocodile, prays to spiders, prays to tortoise, prays to octopus, prays to bats, prays to owl, prays to snails, prays to parrots, prays to penguin, prays to whale, prays to lion, prays to Hippopotamus, prays to all birds, prays to all fishes, Prays to all land animals, Prays to all water animals, prays to all flying animals, prays to all animals, prays to lord Pashupati Nath Paras to do the justice, considering the temple to be the property of country only. Considering the temple to be that system, which generates jobs and revenue for the poor.

In the words of doctors, Shri Rambadan Singh, passed away, on 22nd December 2000. Shri Yougal Kishore Singh passed away on 26th September 2016, Shri Gaya Singh passed away on 7th October 2017, and Shri Sachidanand Singh passed away on 6th February 2023.

Shri Mohandas Karamchand Gandhi passed away on 30 January 1948. Shri Bhagat Singh passed away on 23 March 1931.

> ➤ There is a Proverb, that "Gold got robbed, and the raid on coal".

> ➤ There is another proverb, "Eaten stale chapati".

> ➤ There is another proverb, that "Duryodhan eaten all butter, and left buttermilk for Arjun".

> ➤ There is another proverb, that "Nature and signature, never change".

In the words of Dr. Avul Pakir Jainulabdeen Abdul Kalam Azad, the missile man of India, "FAIL" means, "First attempt in Learning".

Once "Kahoda" was disrespected in the assembly of Raja Janak, and his son "Ashtavakra" having eight bends in his body, was stopped from speaking communicating, or giving knowledge, and were made "mockery" by saying that, now they will give knowledge who themselves need supports to stand properly. It is like, now, they will speak, guide, or will narrate, who themselves "Failed" in the examination. On which, that child, on whose birth, even his father cursed, "Father cursed means, all Devta cursed", asked only one question, that, is this the assembly of "Chamaar", where seeing the body structure, or seeing the color of skin, anyone decided, who is knowledgeable and who is dumb? If this is so, then can understand, that how talented all are. That means toppers were not answering any question raised by "Failure", they were only "tricking and distracting" and making "Mockery" somewhere. It makes "Failures" raise the question, who awarded them "Toppers", who can't even answer any question raised by "Failure"? It's like "Kaurav" having Krishna's, "Narayani Sena".

There is a case of "Mental Harassment" which suits them, who does the "Ascetic" act of blessing, "Malechh, Lafua, Kutta, Maa ki Gaali, Mental, Shuddar, Bhaduwa, Rascal, Fail", it is those family's work, who hurts Ram, because they are "Dancing puppets", and they are those who eat marriage acts, before marriage, somewhere, by their dancing and teasing act, who tries to catch Ram, from birth, like any "Surpankha". Ram means child, especially in the educational system. as in "Kerala" people abuse those trees so that whom, they want to remove them, and that in last, the tree himself dries and falls.

➤ Plantation is the need of the system.

Wherever "Dancing puppets" will be, there will be "Kaamdev". Lord Shiva uses "Ashes" of "Kaamdev" on his forehead, to get relief from stress, or migraine.

Wherever "Dancing puppets" will be, there will be "Ravan". Because he is a very big worshipper of "Lord Shiva". He is expert in "Shiv Tandav Stotram". And the main chanting sacred mantra by those "Ascetic" people is "Malechh, Lafua, Kutta, Shuddar, Maa Ki Gaali, Mental, Fail, Rascal, Bhaduwa, Beggar", using dancing puppets, using girl's father. Marriage is just an illusion somewhere. If suppose, Ram gives gift to any random person, having no daughter, he will complain about giving the gift, as giving and taking gift is also a crime?

Ravan, Daksha, Indra, Kaamdev, Meghnath, Kans, and Shakuni, are addicted to living luxurious life only. If will pull their luxuriousness, then they will die automatically. It is said, whatever is given, is given by Ram, and the rest of others are "Beggar" which means, whatever was with Ravan, Daksha, Indra, Kaamdev, Meghnath, Kans, Shakuni, was given by Ram only, whatever was with them, was because of Ram. And they are those, who trick for making "Ram" into being "Beggar, Vanvaasi, Fakir", which means, they rob "Ram", that much, that "Ram" looks them to be "Vanvaasi, Beggar, Fakir". The moment, Ram left the attachment to the illusion of Sita, Sati, where she topped, and he failed, and married "Parvati", became "Vermilion" of "Parvati", that very moment, Lord Shiva, became the god of all fourteen worlds. Seven upper worlds and seven lower worlds.

➤ What is dancing puppets?

They are only an illusion, which robs sight, property, and respect. There is a movie of Shri Rajesh Khanna, named "Roti" in which a girl was dancing to the song "Dance my dear, you will get money, where will you get such an appreciator", and Shri Rajesh Khanna was robbing. Just imagine the song, "Dance my dear, you will get money, where will you get such an appreciator", where the girl is dancing among children of coeducation, and the girl's father, and brother robbing, those children using their "Dancing puppets".. "Dancing puppets" are illusion. If you are in touch with a girl, then your name will be defamed automatically. They will complain of teasing. They are defaming machines, especially dancing puppets. Because, it's the girl's father's responsibility to marry their girl, not of batchmate, not of society. If anywhere, any rudeness happens to any girl, inside any office, inside any institution, then, behind that, her own family should be accused. Batchmate, society even need, they can't get someone's daughter married, because the daughter's father, even has to touch the groom's feet in marriage. "Vermillion" is not any powder. Whoever breaks this "Law", that means, they are responsible for making "Sati", not that child. And school should not be used as any marriage bureau.

Giving anything to a girl, and expecting her to answer or to reply or to respond, or to give anything in response, is a waste of time. There was a lady who, according to her, no one deserved Bharat Ratan, She awarded herself to be the "Bharat Ratan". She was that much talented. She was not ill, She was very talented, and she awarded herself the "Bharat Ratan". Girl are those things, if given any power, anything, then beg. She is just an illusion only. The moment, she abuses or allows her family to abuse, that very moment, she sowed the seed of "Abhimanyu". Whatever "Arjun" felt, whether "Abhimanyu" will feel the same or not? As, the father, as the child will be or not? Girls are just an illusion. They are that much rich personalities, that on chocolate of rupees five, if will buy any chocolate for them, their father and mother, their brother, will start chanting special mantras "Malechh, Lafua, Kutta, Mental, Maa ki Gaali, Shuddar, Kutta, Rascal, Fail, Bhaduwa, Beggar". They are that much talented. Wherever such abusive behavior happens, that means, the girl was abusing a particular, and was serving respect somewhere else. That means, she was only robbing from one door and was serving somewhere else.

Every school is requested, either to run an educational institution, run a marriage bureau, or run a center for making prostitutes and Bhaduwa. Don't pollute the educational institutions. Wherever there will be dancing activity, that place is doubtful. Who is dancing there? Daughter or mother? Why is she dancing? Only teachers are not witnessing their dances, other batchmates are also witnessing, and are losing lives, and respect. if anywhere, anyone allows any dancing act, then please remove all boys from that place, and let them dance among themselves, and leave themselves to answer, that who was awarding? Whether such a place is any educational institution? It is a "Mujralay" only.

Dancing puppets means a teaser, who teases the most. For example, suppose I am a girl and a dancer, I danced, among 100 students, abused some, appreciated some, shaken body, given signals from hand, given signals from eyebrows, never felt, how others would have felt, as I am a puppet only.

> What is "Shiv Tandav Stotram"?

By mistake, due to addiction to abusing, and robbing, "Daksha, Ravan" did "Kanya Daan" on the head of Lord Shiva become the moon, of lord shiva. Does he look "Malechh, Lafua, Kutta, Maa Ki gaali, Shuddar, Bhaduwa, Fail, Beggar"? Ravan was that much big worshipper of "Lord Shiva". Bramha's great-grandchildren were that much big worshippers of "Lord Shiva". He was such a big worshipper, that, his all children died. He worshipped "Shani Dev" underfoot, and then worshipped lord Shiva with his special chanting mantra, or an Ascetic act. "Ravan", and "Daksha", all expected "Sita", but, Sita/Sati was always found to be their daughter only. Inside police lockup, worship means what? And, "Kanya Daan" is an act of god. Anywhere, if "Love and friendship" dies, then dies due to this special chanting using "Dancing puppets".

> All were to live below the knees, there, who is the moon of lord Shiva?

Suppose, Ram doesn't know "Sita", then, whether anyone has any right to abuse "Ram"? Suppose, Lord Shiva doesn't know "Sati", then whether anyone has any right to abuse "Lord Shiva"?

Whoever was in the place of "Sati", the daughter of "Daksha" was, someone else is "Sati" today, and someone else will be "Sati" tomorrow. Because no one dies ever, no words die ever, no posts die ever. Because of that extraordinary slap and abusive behavior of "Ravan/Daksha". Because even donkeys are reading too. Because copiers are reading too.

Whoever touched the feet of "Ram", inside "Ramayana", they were Safe. Whoever denied it, they died.

Dancing puppets and their guardians should always know, that, inside the same school, or college, where they dance, or sing, there, even teacher's children are also learning to read and write among them. Otherwise, faces of dancing puppets, criminals, robbers, prostitutes, and families would be found to be robbing only from the door of Vishnu, Shiva, and Bramha. Ravan was the servant of Vishnu, story storyteller hired to tell different stories from "Holy Books" to Lord Ganesha, by Lord Shiva. Ram is the face of Vishnu, Ram is the face of "Lord Shiva". The person who was hired and was earning from the door of "Ram', was chopping a knife, somewhere, the coeducation system is that thing, which needs to be checked. Suppose, I am a girl's father, and my daughter is talking with a boy, then also I would know, all, the probabilities. That means, the day, when Ram was given a ring, or chocolate, or any gift, from that day, hiding, using girls, and abusing "Malechh, Lafua, Mental, Kutta, Maa Ki Gaali, Shuddar, Rascal, Fail, Bhaduwa, Beggar". Is this "Devi's door language? It was the girl's mother, who was playing from behind. Coeducation is that thing. because, if in life of over lakhs of children faced the same set of abusive languages, then what should be said to dancing puppets, and those-guardian? Wherever, such seed they were shown, then sown in daughter's life, or daughter's children's life. Why, such extraordinary words arrows are used? Whether in every life, this "Pandit" and "Jajman" theory will happen, or boycott coeducation? Girl was, on the one hand robbing "Raja Vibhuti Narayan", and on the other hand, was calling Shashidhar too. One was "Pandit", and the other was "Jajman".

The child, who yet had not opened his eyes, not yet had crossed "Sataisa", there what is coeducation? Whether tricked for killing or not? Especially by "Dancing Puppets".

Inside "Chhath" pooja, Brahman's are banned, this is that pooja. There is no need of Brahman. What will they do? Nothing to read? Having no "Mantra" for chanting. No "Holy book" to read and that is why somewhere, it is called "Chhath Mahaparv", the Festival, having no existence of Brahman, that Festival is called "Chhath Mahaparv". This is that pooja, which is celebrated after begging, and its prasad is eaten after begging. Chhath pooja is the pooja, mainly celebrated by laborers and the poor, controls lots of diseases, like high blood pressure, diabetes, and others. Poor people celebrate it very happily, even after begging, they celebrate. "Surya Dev" means, the god, who enlightens every home, and watches every act, that is how "Laxmi" designed begging life, and that is how "Sarswati" designed words like "Malechh, Lafua, Kutta, Mental, Maa ki gaali, Shuddar, Bhaduwa, Fail". Or can be said, that this extraordinary system. "Devi Bhumi" notices everything. "Vaayu Dev" notices, Hanuman notices. The child is not in favor of expecting 48% per annum. If he will expect 48% as interest or penalty, then, what was that poor selling?

Boycott coeducation, because even girls are also faces of Barbarik, on the one hand, they call "Love" too, and even calls "Jajman" too, and use their father to slap, them for doing the "Kanya Daan" on the head. Shared my experience, as any school shares their experience while designing mark sheets and certificates for their work, in the same way, he shared his experience.

The child pulls all power of "Ravan, Kans, Shakuni, Meghnath, Daksha" chop their hand, chops their tongue, chops their legs, chops their all weapons, used for robbing, and the "Kanya Daan" on their head, becomes peacock's leaf of lord Vishnu, moon of Lord Shiva.

Girls should always keep in mind, that, whatever their family background, whatever their report card, but that doesn't allow them to disrespect anyone. Because the trees have fruits on them, they by nature bend. Their steam by nature bends. With great power, great responsibility comes.

Wherever, any girl gets gifted inside the educational system, there, their father should do some kindness, by moving towards that child's home, to see his nature. If searching groom, sitting from home, then, that means, spoiling the daughter's life too. because, the child who gifted, doesn't know, that their daughter is only a puppet or an illusion. The children who gifted anything don't know, that their fathers are waiting for their family members to die, their fathers are waiting for their retirement, their father had invested their money in their batchmate's home, and are waiting for that money to be returned on 48% per year, so that, their daughter's would be married fanfare, and happily. Which spoils, her and other's time too. Fighting with which brother? According to "Devi Ji", "India is her country, and all Indians are her brothers and sisters", there which Brothers are "Malechh, Lafua, Kutta, Mental, Maa Ki Gaali, Shuddar, Fail, Rascal, Bhaduwa, Beggar"? The coeducational system is the system, which somewhere is a doubtful place, where, "Meghnath, Kans, Shakuni, Ravan" gets benefited somewhere. Or can be said, that, "Meghnath, Kans, Shakuni, Ravan" all have chosen a coeducational system, for finding a groom, secretly, hiding from home. "Meghnath, Kans, Shakuni, Ravan" are those begging characters, about whom can't say anything. When it is said, that "Data ek Ram Bhikhaari Saari Duniya", then, the chapati in Ravan's, Meghnath, Kan's home, was also coming from Ram's home only. They are those, who eat on whichever plate, will be found making holes in that plate only.

Girl fathers are that important in the marriage act, blessing of a girl's mother is also that much needed. But, were disrespecting and disrespecting, because of having the blessing right, but, blessing right changes place. "Staff" were improper, they were those literate, who were checking the power of reading and writing, complaining, ordering, and suggesting, in writing somewhere. That is why, maybe people expect children to become writers. A single complaint over a certificate, experience, or character, spoils all past, in present, and affects the future having any certificate, post, or character. There, he was expected to give in writing, somewhere, as a part of "Ragging", just because was in the coeducation system, somewhere, where, "Draupadi/Sati" lies. Draupadi means, either the groom dies or the child dies. As, wherever "Arjun" was earlier, there even "Abhimanyu" was to be there. Sati, means, the coconut, which is neither to be eaten for "Pandit", nor for "Jajman" established during Durga puja over the "Kalash", because she was giving signals to more than one person, somewhere, at a time. "Love" is provoked by girls, not imposed by boys. Marriage is that act, where even a girl's father has to touch their groom's feet.

The groom, should have the right to slap the girl's brother too, if any girl's father, has any right to slap and abuse, then whether the groom has the same right or not?

Clap doesn't happen, with one hand, for clapping, both hands have equal effort. "Love" is always provoked by the girl, and not can be imposed by anyone. And coeducation system is a system, which is not any system. The girl, herself is the face of "Surpankha", the girl herself are face of "Sorsa", girl herself is the face of their father, who from behind, suggests, and uses, their girl's faces. And eats children's lives and time somewhere.

Suppose a child, having no degree, wrote a story with over a hundred pages, which has buyers, then what will degree holders do? Can read only. Having the same human rights. On whichever post, degree holders will be, they are only supposed to read only.

If any child is a writer, then whether he need any degree? If any child wrote his "Mann ki Baat", or "Answered in his own words", then whether anyone has any problem? If any child is the manufacturer of "Books" then did anything wrong? What is the degree for this child? How many days, can anyone make eclipse on any child, using "Dancing puppets"? A child passed in 2015, but his mark sheet and certificate were still pending to be given in 2024. Whether eaten his right or not, if not awarded him his mark sheet and certificate, even after eight written applications. Is the fee a "Service charge" or not? Which "Service" do they give? Whether, if the child will protest, then will call the police or not? Whether they provoke or not to students, with the services, they give?

All are acting child, living the life of after "Jenau", and hiding their past, that is why "Jenau" held, with their present, with their children. Before "Jenau" they were "Maa Ki Gaali", and after "Jenau" they became "Bhaduwa", before "Jenau", they were "Shuddar", and after "Jenau", they became "Bhaduwa", which means, "Jenau" is that proof, where someone robbed them, and abused them in all aspects, keeping the girl ahead, they were abusing him and were disrespecting. Inside the marriage act, the girl has no right to speak. The groom touched the feet, father-in-law touched the feet. In between these two steps, whether anyone has any right to slap, and abuse? It is like robbing the groom and bride too.

"Love" and "Devi" are those things, who from birth, they are those things, that will beat you, and will abuse you and your husband. The child swears, that his child will not choose any coeducational system.

> ➤ Whether these two children, needs to become any "Bhaduwa" before marriage?

As, before "Jenau", they are "Shuddar", and after "Jenau" they are "Bhaduwa". Whether these children need to become any "Bhaduwa" before marriage? Or girl father, will learn to respect them? whether they "Failed"? To understand, what is the "coeducational system"? And which life those were living, who were living the life of after "Jenau".

➤ What is "Jenau"?

It is just an act of robbing the child's shield. Before "Jenau" he is "Shuddar" and after "Jenau" he is "Bhaduwa". Who is running this extraordinary purifying agency? "Jenau" may be necessary, but it should not be considered to be any necessary act. It should be only an act of worship, for "Ram" only.

Shields are robbed because, under that shield, lots of ornaments are, by-birth, and for robbing those ornaments are robbed somewhere, by them, whomever "Ram" trusted. Virtue is robbed. Surya Dev would know better, and Devi Bhumi would know better.

Wherever such things happen, that, first "Chumaan" will occur, then "Jenau" will occur, they are neither of "Love" nor of any "Holy books". That means, wherever, such things happen, that first "Love" will occur, then a breakup will happen, then, surgery will happen, they are neither of "Love" nor of any "Holy book". That means they are those laundry dogs, neither of home nor of Ghat. They are those talented girls.

In the construction of human, horses have even given their contribution, and if the horse has any friendship with grasses, then will eat what?

I pray to all planets, Mercury, Venus, Earth, Mars, Jupiter, Saturn, Uranus, Neptune, and Pluto. I Prays to all stars, Sun, Methuselah, UY Scuti, considering them to be fixed, around whom all their children planets are revolving, that whoever disrespects any member of Brahman Bharadwaj Bhumihaar, or tricking any member of Brahman Bharadwaj Bhumihaar", using someone else face, or using even Brahman Bharadwaj Bhumihaar for disrespecting, or for provoking to disrespect, make them "Landless, Powerless, Speechless, tongueless, Handless, Jobless, legless, toothless, Navel less" in all aspects.

I pray, that, to any "Ram", in any birth, "Sita's" mother, or girl's father, doesn't ever call first.

And the act of "Jenau" should be considered to be an act of "Pin drop silent" only. Should not affect any Ram, or child. They should be expected to give in writing, that what happened, as the sensor lies all where. Because the child has the right to pull in feet, only after touching father-in-law's feet. Ram should be safe, in all aspects. "Love" can happen, only after touching the feet of the groom. And girls will have to touch their guardian's feet, elder brother's feet, then "Grandfather-in-law's" feet, "Father-in-law's" feet, then the groom's feet. There is a function of reception, after which the bride touches the groom's feet. There what is "Love"? Inside marriage, girls are taught, to eat a piece of stale food too. Cow dung is thrown over the girl's brother.

Whoever founds reading this book, prays to Goddess Laxmi, Goddess Saraswati, Goddess Durga, and Goddess Kali, for their happy and prosperous life, and their honest works.

No one can ban any book, Bible, Quran, or Ramayana, all are books having different variables. And children go or come to school to become writers only. The writer even does their "Mann Ki Baat", which means they "Answers in their own words" only. They are not any copiers, or Xerox printers. If anyone needs only words from "Book", then take the "Open book test". It is also in the system. As they are paying the fees.

Writing is also an Ascetic act, awarded "FAIL", and Mr. Bamula died. Uses someone else mouth, for their word arrow. Uses someone else mouth for saying "Malechh, Lafua, Kutta, Shuddar, Maa Ki Gaali, Mental, Fail, Rascal, Bhaduwa, Beggar". "Lotus" grows in mud, and in "Laxmi puja" "Lotus flower" are dedicated to goddess "Laxmi" and her brother "Lord Ganesha" in "Dipawali".

It is like, a person went to a funeral, and there, he was given some sweets to eat. The person asked them with sorrow, how they died. The family members with full politeness, replied, that, they had "Diabetes", and in their memory, we are serving "Sweets". In the same way, maybe in the memory of some legends, "FAIL" is awarded. At least they learned something.

"I Love You" is also an Ascetic act, where someone else from behind uses someone else face or mouth to use the phrase "I Love You", provoked by someone. Whoever founds to be using the same phrase over one girl, please make them "Landless, Speechless, Powerless, Handless, Tongueless, Teethless, Navel less". If love held, then marry them.

Whoever founds robbing "Bharat, Hindustan, India", whoever found robbing "Devi Bhumi", founds robbing ornaments of "Devi Bhumi", Please chop their "Hand, legs, tongues" and make them "Landless".

Once Hirnayakashyapu, beaten his child, tied him to a pillar and beaten him, and used "Holika", to kill him.

Once Lord Ganesha, stopped the path of Lord Shiva, as he was Parvati's "Driver, Guard, Peon, Accountant, Treasure". Lord Shiva chopped Lord Ganesha's head. After that, Lord Shiva became the guard of that head. Guardian's beating, means, sculpture creating something.

For every child, her mother, remains beautiful, without even "Make-up".

Writing is an Art, where words are assembled, where words are decorated, for playing with the eyeballs, ears, and sentiments of readers. Students give their effort, and for that, grace will be the student's right. Grace means, at least, they given them a chance to live, to live in that field or sector, considering them, to have some learning during the sessions. Otherwise, among 50-100 students, who is there, who knows them, among the country having a population of more than one thirty crore. Who "Failed" there?

An Indian engineer designed "Vande Bharat Express", while reaching his retirement. What was his result during schooling, and college, that was of no use. If a person designs a Drone or flying Machine, what was his result during schooling, or college, that was of no use. A person-designed computer, what was his result over any piece of paper during schooling, colleges, was of no use.

Keeping animals is a virtuous thing. They are a very good friend of children, guardians, and family members. They, take every curse over their family over them, whenever needed. Someone earned a curse of over lakhs of leeches, for their act, a puppy taken over them, for saving them. Animals are real well-wishers of humans. Animals are also mammals. I have seen a puppy sitting around a cow with discipline for cow to give milk. Animals have their bonding with each other. Humans got human rights, from animals, animals can't write.

Has anyone noticed or not, that mother, and grandmother, cooking extra chapati for birds in their home? Has anyone noticed or not, that mother, grandmother, used to give milk to cats too, though having a dog in the home, even after that she keeps "Milk" there too. In their blessing, god lies. In their blessing, god lies. Because they can't milk any cow. In the same way, grand guardians are, even their time has value.

Special thanks to Shrimati Rajrani Madam, Shrimati Padma Madam, Shrimati Shailbaala Madam, Shrimati Bharti Madam, Shri Paul Sir, Shri Raman Sir, Shri Krishna Prakash Sir, Shri Krishna Pandey Sir, Shri Ramvilas Vidyarthi Sir, Shri Nageshwar Sir, Shri Antaryaami Sir, Shri Gopal Sir, Shri Abhay Sir, Shri Rajeev Ranjan Sinha Sir, Shri N.K Jha sir, Shri Lalit Ghoswami Sir, Shrimati Madhu Madam, Shrimati Sangeeta Sundar, Shrimati Vibha Sharma, Shrimati Vaijanti Mala, Shrimati Madhvi Singh, Shri Lalit Choudhary Singh, Shri Chandra Sir, Shri Gupta Sir, Shrimati Buddhiya Devi, Shri Raghunath Prasad Sharma, Shri Manohar Pandey, Shri Dharmendra Sir, Shri Devashish Sir, Shri Rajeev Ranjan sir, Shri Shankar Singh, Shri Abhay Sir, Shri Kumar Pushpanjay sir, Shri Bhupendra Soam Sir, Shri Saurabh Mittal Sir, Shrimati Bhajneet Kaur Madam,

Shrimati Namita Dixit Madam, Shri Rajni Joshi Madam, Shri Vijesh Jain, Shri Arun Sangwan, Shrimati Suchi Dixit madam, Madam Farida Rasiwala, Shrimati Manpreet uppal, Shri Manpreet Sandhu, Dr. Rini Bhagaur, Shri Shashi Bharti, Dr. Samridhi Bhatia, Shri R.K Shrivastava, Shrimati Radhika Shrivastava, Shri Anil Kumar Sinha, Shrimati Purnima Rao, Shrimati Ahuja Madam, Shri Neel Sir, Shri Ramesh Sir, Shri Robin Sir, Shrimati Kshamta Chauhan, and other teaching and non-teaching faculties.

Special thanks to Shri Suresh Prasad Sinha, Shri Raghvendra Kumar, Shri Dev Karan Singh, Shri Sanjeet Prasad Sinha, Shri Shubham Kumar, Shri Prashant Prasad Sinha, Shri Raj Kumar, Shri Ravinder rai, Shri Virender Rai, Shri Murli Sharma, Shri Shambhu Rai, Shri Krishna cant Shahi, Shri Lokesh Prasad Sinha, Shri Krishna Singh, Shri Devender Rai, Shri Pramod Shahi, Shri U.N Choudhary, Shri Padan Narayan Singh, Shri Anant Thakur, Shri Bachchu Singh, Shri Vijay Singh, Shri Manoj Roy, Shri Umesh Kumar Singh, Shri Surrender Kumar, Shri Arvind Sharma, Shri Arvind Kumar, Shri Nirmal Singh, Shri Vinay Singh, Shri Mukesh choudhary.

He thanked them, who appreciated him with words like "Rajendra Kumar and Shahrukh" because no one could look at his face, by himself. It's they who reply. Or keep watching the mirror, the mirror will never reply.

He thanks Shri Krishna Singh, Shri Ajit Singh, Shri Krishna Cant Sahi, Shri Lokesh Prasad Sinha, Shri Bachchu Singh, Shri Pandan Narayan Singh, Shri U.N Choudhary, Shri Anant Thakur, Shri

Vijay Singh, Shri Manoj Roy, Shri Surrender Kumar, Shri Mrityunjay Singh, Shri Umesh Kumar Singh, Madam Shivaagami, Shri M. Sundar, Shri Thiru, Shri Kumaresan, Shri Alagappa Chityaar, Shri Thanthai Periyar, Dr. A. Shanmugasundaram and others.

Special thanks to Navjeet, Sujit, Rohit, Atin, and Dheeraj for their presence.

Special thanks to "Kiran, Glory, Rupa Sharma, and Simran", for their extraordinary presence, in the direction of Bramha and Saraswati somewhere, using dancing puppets, especially having a scar or mole on the face. Who was busy in answering with her posing nature, by the direction of suggestion makers. Suggestion makers were using her, for robbing them only. Every suggestion, every appreciation, is not "Nectar".

- There is a song "Hey man, watch while walking, not only ahead, but also see the back, while walking, not only to right but also to left, not only to high up in the air but also see down to earth."

- There is a song "Start the Generator, and Watch the Theatre".

- There is another song "Oh, my dear, Johrajbeen, you don't knows, that you are still a beautiful, and I am still young".

- There is another song, "Oh, where will you go away, after being annoyed by me? Wherever will go, will find me only".

- There is another song "Bob dropped in the market of Bareilly".

- There is another song "Aching heart, Aching liver, you woke in the heart, and I wrote the same, whatever you asked me to write".

- There is another song, "Whatever you like, will speak the same, if will ask to say night to day, then will speak night only."

- There is another song, "My heart is mental, who loves you, but whenever you comes in front of me, fears of speaking anything".

Thank you

54UR48H M4F14.
XYZ.

www.ingramcontent.com/pod-product-compliance
Lightning Source LLC
Chambersburg PA
CBHW031146130726
47988CB00006B/2563